CW01500967

Who Said Life Should Be Easy?

By

Linda Durman

ISBN: 978-1-9163097-6-0

Published By: -

i2i Publishing. Manchester.

www.i2ipublishing.co.uk

For my talented and exceptional children,
Alex and JoKate

Acknowledgement

Written with thanks to my current husband, with whom I have shared much of the fun and who has supported and cared for me for forty years; that hasn't always been easy either!

Contents

Prologue

What to leave out?

During the centenary of the First World War, I shared stories of my grandfather's war. He was a gentle man, and I didn't want his story to be lost, so I wrote some of it down. Then I wrote about Nanna, his wife, who adored me and my brother, David and from whom we got unconditional love. Nanna had a huge influence on me as I was growing up. This Is how the book started.

I have always enjoyed writing, starting with letters to pen friends and a family magazine, through endless exams at school and university. Almost all my NHS work in Public Health resulted a written report. This required an impersonal style that was hard to shrug off when I turned to creative writing. Like many people, I have always believed that there is a book in me, but only short stories took shape. Then I read that the first novel is almost always a form of autobiography, so I decided to write one to get that out of the way.

I was born gifted with the belief that whatever happens, I would be alright. When opportunities opened up for me, I nearly always took the path that looked most interesting rather than the one that looked safe. There are always people around who will point out the risks for you, aren't there? As a consequence, I have often been frightened but never bored.

During my formative years, like all children of the 1950s I was socialised to conform; to obey the rules. Never actually spoken, the impression I got was that having been born illegitimate I had further to climb to become socially acceptable and should be extra careful not to stand out. Of course, I kept forgetting, but on the whole, I remained a sweet, biddable young woman until two things happened: the sixties and my son. Having started along the road of medical training, I remained careful not to upset any apple carts that would prejudice my career but became a raging tiger if any prejudice was aimed at my son. I soon learnt that standing up to bullies and prejudice suited me, and despite feeling a bit panicky at the time, I soon felt stronger for doing and saying the right thing. This stood me in good stead for the future.

Some of the chapters were hard to write. The anguish of failed marriages and separation from my children was no easier fifty years later. There have been times in life when I felt very low, but the key is to just keep going. And to read Scott Peck, whose philosophy is that we are not here to be happy; we are here to learn. Happiness is just a by-product of the way we live our lives.

One of the hardest things writing a memoir is deciding what to leave out. I started by including stories about all the inspirational women in my life, and how important they have been to me. I soon came to the conclusion that this would be another whole book. I also decided to leave out a lot of juicy bits, because they are none of your business.

Since I retired from paid work, I spend more time with friends. Unlike our parents' generation, most of us (women) have had careers as professionals but we rarely see our experiences written down or talked about. Oft times we are introduced to new people as 'my wife'. The next step in the conversation is usually one of the men asking the other 'what did you do?' meaning, what job did you do before retirement. Men of our generation never ask this of the women they meet.

They are missing some interesting stuff, some of which follows.

Chapter 1

An adopted alien?

Cunningly, I delayed being born until the war was over and by the age of two, I had also avoided deportation to the colonies and been the subject of a forced adoption. Actually, missing the Second World War was intensely annoying, because it was all anyone talked about for years.

I was born illegitimate in September 1945. In 1940s England, the social stigma of having a child out of wedlock was such that a woman ran the risk of being disowned by her family. Alone, she would struggle to find rented accommodation or employment. Many families dealt with an unwanted pregnancy by grafting the unplanned baby onto another family group to be brought up by grandparents or older siblings. As I later discovered, my birth mother's family was not so helpful. Her father turned her out of the house, and she went to a mother and baby home in Tunbridge Wells to have her baby. After six weeks, she had to leave and return to London and her secretarial job while I stayed at the home.

My mother visited once a week, bringing with her some ill-fitting baby clothes and my ration coupons, but when I started to crawl, she was told that I couldn't stay at the home any longer and she would have to choose between caring for me herself and having me adopted. Her work in London hardly paid enough to cover her keep and the train fare to Kent and so with great misgivings, she agreed that I should be considered for adoption. It was not unusual for judgemental attitudes to result in social pressure on single women to give up their child for adoption. She would probably not have been informed about the welfare services that were available at the time including housing and financial help. As a result, women like my mother did not give what we would now regard as informed consent to the adoption. This situation has been called forced adoption.

New parents

In 1942, Betty and Bernard got married. The war was still on and they were posted to Shawlands in Glasgow. By 1945, they decided they had waited long enough for children and perhaps it was not going to happen. A family friend, Mabel Slaughter, knew of a mother and baby home in Kent where many of the babies were available for adoption. She also had a car which was quite unusual in 1946, so Mabel drove Betty down there to have a look. I am told that I sat up in my pram, sunlight glancing off my blond curls and greeted Betty and Mabel with a broad smile. Apparently, this was quite unlike me as I was usually a quiet serious child, who rarely gave away a smile for free.

Some weeks later, just before Betty and Bernard came to collect me and take me home, I developed chickenpox. In order to keep me looking saleable, someone at the home picked the huge scabs off my face and disguised them with makeup. This achieved the level of appeal required and I was taken home by Betty to wait out the adoption process. The pox scars on my face eventually healed but left one or two permanent reminders.

There were a lot of spare babies in 1946; some orphans, some just born to mothers who hadn't expected them. A quarter of all births were illegitimate that year, which was considered shocking. Adoption had been invented in 1926 as a means of 'providing relief for unmarried mothers and satisfying the needs of those couples unable to conceive themselves.' The interests of the children were not taken into consideration. Nor were the responsibilities of the absent fathers. In the five years after World War Two, babies were being adopted at a rate of about 18,000 a year. Adoption was often arranged for a fee by a private individual rather than a registered agency until the Adoption of Children Act 1949 ensured that placement of children for adoption would be the responsibility of local authorities. Despite the increased number of adoptions, there were many more babies than adopters. This was partly due to the serious shortage of housing and the fact that men recently returned from the war were starting their own families. I was one of the lucky ones who found a family.

Since I was completely unaware of any of this, I settled nicely into my new home. We lived in Wembley with Betty's parents, Nanna and Pop. I always knew that I had been adopted. It felt normal. Your mum and dad and brother are your mum and dad and brother, just like everyone else. But there were things about it that were not normal. People would look at me when they heard I was adopted, as if they suddenly weren't sure about me. And then, there would be an awkward conversation, after which mum would say, 'don't tell people; we like to think of you as our own,' which would set me wondering about who I really was.

When I was little, I sometimes fantasised about being a princess who had to be shielded from publicity for my own safety. Or maybe the daughter of a serial killer that they couldn't tell me about, even an alien from another planet. It perplexed me. Children who know that they are adopted often have feelings of worthlessness and get depressed, especially during teenage years. My disposition was altogether different from that. The most common word used to describe me was placid or in school reports 'intelligent, with a well-developed imagination.' In general, I just fitted in and did not make a fuss unless confronted by a situation in which someone was being treated unfairly, when I would fly into an uncharacteristic rage in their defence.

Chapter 2

Why not boys' toys?

Everything was scarce and rationed after the Second World War but ex-soldiers such as my dad had priority for housing and in 1948, we moved into a new semi-detached house in Thorpe Bay in Essex. Like all our houses, this was named Shawlands. Nanna and Pop also moved from Wembley to a house along our road.

Along that road, a rush of younger children was born straight after the war, keeping our mothers busy and allowing us older children more freedom. We made noisy convoys by joining our bikes, trikes and wooden trucks with string. Few people had their own car and it was safe to play for hours on the wide pavements.

Down the road, beside Nanna and Pop's house, was the horse field with a ramshackle stable made from corrugated iron where the rag and bone man kept his horse. This field was our territory. We whittled pea shooters, bows, arrows and catapults for fierce wars against imagined enemies. I was the only girl in the gang and the boys assumed I would not be as good as them. I worked out how to be the best; climbing further, throwing longer, running faster.

From my bedroom window, I watched wheat being planted, grown and harvested. The wheat was stacked to dry in hay ricks until the farmer bought a combine harvester. This was a significant local event, and everyone went out to watch it. Keith, next door, was three years old and could draw the combine harvester with total accuracy from memory. I was impressed, as I was six and had no aptitude for drawing, colouring in or painting. Keith's extraordinary drawing powers somehow explained why he was too clever to pay any attention to normal lessons when he went to school.

The best part of the combine harvester's arrival was its ability to make square straw bales that were built into tall haystacks, whose main purpose was clearly to provide the set for games of Cowboys and Indians. There was time for hunting lizards in the drainage trenches around the fields but I had to be careful not to catch them by the tail or they would just shed it and run away, leaving me desolate that I had deprived a potential pet of an important part of itself. However much anyone told you that he would grow a new tail, I still knew he would be upset. On the far side of the big fields were tall elms full of noisy birds and their nests. Beyond those trees was the world. We didn't venture that far.

My parents complained about the boxes and bottles in the garage in which I kept lizards, tadpoles and the chrysalises that would become butterflies and moths. Sometimes, we staged a war against the children who lived near the shops. We called them 'the bullybunnies.' The war consisted mainly of hiding, shouting and badly aimed catapults. None of this sat well with mum who was trying to improve me. She despaired over dolls that were not played with and my muddy torn clothes. I was perplexed even then because boys never seemed to get in trouble for being muddy.

A new brother
Although we were not at all well-off, I was sent to a private school, ballet classes and elocution lessons. Nothing worked. What I really wanted was Lego or a huge Mechano set. On the odd occasion when I tried to join in and make things with someone else's construction kit, an adult would

try to dissuade me with the explanation that these were boys' toys.

My brother was born in January 1949. I wanted to call him Chrysanthemum, but this did not catch on. They called him David John. He was a fragile baby and took a long time to gain any weight. I think he probably had pyloric stenosis. It was clear that he wouldn't be climbing trees or making catapults any time soon.

While mum was pregnant and when David was small, I spent much of my time four doors down with Nanna and Pop. I loved Nanna. David and I were the light of her life. When I tore my clothes climbing trees, she patched them up - many of them she had made herself, but she didn't get cross. Some of Nanna's family were tailors in Leicester so she knew about sewing and taught me. In fact, I can't remember a time before I was able to sew. For a while, Nanna worked in a small dressmaking business and brought the off-cuts home for me to make dolls' clothes. Every Christmas, I was the first to stir her Christmas pudding mix and make a wish, because the first wish always comes true. Nanna never doubted that I could achieve whatever I wanted. I loved her house because it was calm. No-one lost their temper there or sulked. There were no long silences or screaming matches. I often wondered how she and Pop could have a daughter with a personality so different from their own.

Nanna's father had been a pioneer in the early days of indoor plumbing around 1900, when ordinary people began to invest in the novelty of an indoor toilet. He was a good plumber, but a poor businessman and their family life swung between having plenty of money, then somehow not have any because the business had lost it all. When they were down on their luck, Nanna's mother would sell twists of tea to make ends meet. Nanna's eldest sister, the formidable Auntie Ethel, managed to get an education and become a schoolteacher in the 1920s. She used to tell how some of her pupils were sewn into their underclothes for the winter.

Nanna's other sister, Auntie May, used to collect rainwater in a zinc bath and heat it in the kitchen for my small brother to bathe in. She firmly believed this would rid him of eczema. Unlike Auntie Ethel, Auntie May and Nanna did not benefit from higher education because there wasn't enough money around at the time. May married George, who was also a plumber but with significantly more business acumen than her father and a profound understanding of physics. In the mid-20th century, his company expanded from domestic plumbing to commercial work, designing and building machinery for a factory that made jam. This impressed me no end.

Medal winner with seven brothers

Even when I was small, I knew that Pop was very deaf from explosions in the First World War trenches and that I should speak clearly and make sure he could see my lips move. He would never talk about his time as a soldier in World War One and how he got a medal, but I did once see the scar behind his knee where a bullet went through. Nanna said it happened when he was recovering a friend who had been shot and was lying on a hillside. Pop got a medal.

Pop had seven brothers, so he probably knew what it was going to be like when he went to war. He was not a fighting sort of man. He joined the Sherwood Foresters in

1917 when he was eighteen. They sent him to France where he fought at Ypres and the battle of the Somme. Nanna said he would never eat curry after that, because they used curry powder to disguise the rotten meat the British soldiers had to eat in France. She said he was gassed too, so he shouldn't really smoke. I hated the smell of cigarettes on people, but on Pop it seemed natural. He was the only person I ever bought cigarettes for, on the basis that there wasn't much else that he liked for Christmas and they hadn't done him any apparent harm for sixty years.

Being a soldier in the First World War was awful. Pop decided that the horror would stop with him. If he did not talk about his war, we would not hear about it and the horror would not penetrate our imagination or haunt our nights. Nanna must have heard stories about how it was at the Somme and how bad it had been, because so many of the men she knew, including Pop's brother Ernest, did not come back and many who did come back were maimed. We were similarly gentle with Uncle Will, Pop's brother who lost an arm in that war. Since Nanna and Pop were the most important people in my life, the gentleness of their presence and the underlying reason for it, had a profound effect on me as I was growing up.

Pop was a quiet man, not given to expressing his views. Maybe that explained why everyone liked him and treated him gently. By the time he got to be my granddad, he had founded a cricket club in Wembley and been President of the Wembley Ratepayers' Association. He worked for the North British Rubber Company for fifty-two years. When I was a teenager, he was their provincial representative for footwear. Sometimes, I would help with his paperwork, sort out the samples for a new range and type up the wholesale and retail prices for him. He wouldn't type – it was something women did. Actually, he was pretty rigid about what he wouldn't do: he would never push a pram with a baby in it or carry a bunch of flowers, both being deemed too embarrassing. I didn't really understand it and he couldn't explain it. He was also a Freemason. Nanna explained that this was one way he kept in touch with comrades from the First World War. He definitely enjoyed the social occasions there and once came home so drunk that he was sick out of the train window and lost his false teeth.

'He was asking for you this afternoon'
When he was fifty, Pop had to learn to drive in order to keep his job. He hated driving and was the worst driver in the world. He didn't understand the car at all and Nanna, who had hoped to benefit from an occasional outing, was at first disappointed and then relieved that the car would only ever be used for work.

Pop loved his garden. I always thought it was because the plants didn't expect conversation from him. I liked being around him because he didn't ask the stupid questions most grownups did like 'how are you getting on at school?' or 'have you finished your homework?' I would creep down his garden path and he would smile from inside with his eyes and say, 'how do,' then get on with the gardening. He let me help putting stuff on the bonfire and digging. Neither of us cared about getting mud on our clothes and he wouldn't think about whether it was wise to let me use secateurs or carry heavy stuff. Nanna would come out with a cup of tea and homemade biscuits and say 'hi! Look at the state you two are in' and Pop would wink at me and we'd smile and then Nanna would smile, and it would be alright. Some weekends in the summer, we would go to watch cricket at West Kent cricket ground where Pop and I helped with the scores. Pop wrote them down in pencil in a wooden hut and I changed the number of runs on the metal plates hung on the outside.

Apart from gardening, Pop was the least capable person I ever knew. He knew nothing about money, so he let Nanna deal with all that and my dad filled in their tax returns. Pop was hopeless around the house, and there was a constant to-ing and fro-ing of neighbours and friends to help fix things. I don't think he could even change a fuse. My dad did all their decorating. When Nanna went into hospital one time, mum had to prepare all Pop's meals and do the washing. Towards the end of the second week, she asked why there wasn't any underwear with the washing. 'I don't know where Dorrie keeps my vests and pants,' he said.

Pop had few ambitions apart from a keen desire to achieve his eightieth birthday. When he did, he had a party and was bursting with pride. He died quite soon after that. Mum phoned me to tell me. 'He was asking for you this afternoon,' she said.

When my milk teeth fell out and the new ones grew, I had the biggest gap between my two front teeth that has ever been seen. I could get a half crown, an old threepenny piece and a sixpence between them. I thought this quite smart, but the dentist convinced my mum that they should be straightened. Straightening sounds, well, straightforward. But it is not. It involves impressions, a plastic plate with wires, way too much dental hygiene for anyone with a social life, and ulcers. In addition to which, I had been reliably informed by several grownups that a gap between my two front teeth meant that I was going to marry money. If I closed the gap, did that mean I wouldn't?

In truth, it wasn't a natural gap, but one I had engineered by Olympic thumb sucking at night until I was eleven. Nevertheless, I was left with some concern that when the brace closed the gap, it would compromise my financial future. Up to then, money and I had not had much to do with each other except when sweets came off ration when I was eight, and I celebrated by stealing half a crown from the small change dad left on the dresser every night. He noticed. I enjoyed the sweets but couldn't share the experience and felt very guilty.

In the summer, our family shared a beach hut with four other families. Betty had a baby seat on the back of her bike for David, and I cycled beside them along Southchurch Boulevard to the beach. She taught me to swim in the sea and on weekends, when the dads were also there, we played endless games of beach cricket. When the tide went out you could walk out on the Thames Estuary mud and watch people digging for lugworms for bait. We could see the Kent coast and a lump of the Mulberry Harbour that had not made it to France. I used to stare at it a lot, trying to work out why they expected such a huge lump of concrete to float. We could walk for a mile along the beach to Southend, but not very far the other way towards Shoeburyness, because it was fenced off with barbed wire by the Ministry of Defence. The beach there was mined during the war against invasion and they still had not cleared the mines when we left in 1954.

I wasn't sent to the local school. Betty wanted the best, which to her, meant private school so I was sent to

Lindisfarne Preparatory. This involved a bus ride from Thorpe Bay to the centre of town in Southend, then another bus to Westcliff. For a couple of terms, mum came with me, then I was allowed to go alone. On my first day at school, all the other children cried when their mothers left. I did not. It was disconcerting being surrounded by a mass of inconsolable, drippy children. The school was run by an order of Catholic nuns with Mother Leone as head teacher, who, instead of asking us to tidy up, always said 'a place for each thing and each thing in its place.' It later emerged that few of the nuns had received any teacher training. I was naughty. I stole biscuits from other children's pockets in the cloakroom, took peashooters into class and did brilliant impersonations of Mother St Mary when I thought she wasn't there (she was, in fact, in the stationery cupboard. I was in deep trouble).

We got our first TV in 1953 to watch the Coronation of Queen Elizabeth. It had a tiny black and white picture behind a bulging glass screen, so that we all had to peer very carefully to see anything. That year, a huge crowd of family and friends gathered to watch the Grand National on this new TV. We all 'had a flutter.' My horse won. I was ecstatic, until they told me that I had only won some money, not the horse. I cried, partly because I really wanted the horse and partly from embarrassment.

Mum and dad had both been in an amateur dramatic society in Wembley when they were younger, and later joined the Borough Players in Southend, an amateur theatre group of happy but noisy people glad that the war was over and with hardly any spare cash. Most of the plays were by Noel Coward. Mum came alive on stage. Dad preferred making the scenery and props. He would cut and screw frames together in the back garden because they were too big for either the house or the garage, then nail on canvas ready for painting. Dad's workbench at the back of the garage had shelves he had made himself, underneath which hung dozens of Brylcream jars, their metal lids nailed to the bottom of a shelf. They contained an extremely neat selection of nails and screws. We were allowed to admire but not touch, children being insufficiently orderly.

Most of mum and dad's friends were from the Borough Players, the closest being Arthur and Doris. We all went on holiday together. Arthur was tremendous fun with an irreverent humour. He had a sweet shop on the seafront at Thorpe Bay and sold trays of tea and biscuits for people to take on the beach. When his warehouse caught fire, he lost all his stock. He was not insured. This financial disaster was the main topic of conversation for days in our house. 'Why don't you give him some of our money if he needs it?' I asked. Mum's mouth dropped open and she had a rare moment being lost for words. There was, of course, no answer. This was when they realised that I had not yet fully grasped the concept of capitalism.

Two years later, we moved to Kent. Expecting to go into year three at the local state school, we were shocked to find that I would be in year four and have to take the eleven plus in a few months. I was nine years old and understood that this was bad news. At this new school, it became clear that I had little knowledge apart from details of all the saints and the plight of the poor children in Africa. Betty bought me test papers for the eleven plus which I devoured, so that fortunately, when the eleven plus came, I did pass and went to Grammar School.

Chapter 3

The family taboos

Dad's Royal Army Pay Corps uniform was kept hanging in my wardrobe for many years because he needed to be ready, if called up. Every morning, before he left to catch the train from Thorpe Bay to London, he would clean and polish shoes for the whole family then rake out the ashes, bring in coal and leave a fire set and ready to light. On winter evenings, he hooked hearth rugs to protect the carpet from sparks and 'did the books' for local clubs that had discovered he was an accountant. On Fridays, he brought mum a box of Roses chocolates.

I always knew that dad loved me very much. You can tell from someone's eyes, can't you? He wore heavy, old-fashioned spectacles with thick lenses. When he gave me a hug, he hugged me so tight that it hurt. I don't think he had had the usual lessons on how to show someone that you care for them deeply. Dad could tackle almost any DIY job. In later life, I would be amazed that there were men (husbands) who did not have these DIY skills.

Like all fathers, he seemed hugely tall and strong when I was a child but reduced to a normal size when I reached my teens. He worked as an accountant for Binder Hamlyn and later, as the accountant for Christ's Hospital School. He looked so smart when he went to work in his pin stripe suit and rolled umbrella. In 1950, he tore a cartilage in his knee and had to be helped home from Thorpe Bay station. He had to go up and down stairs on his bum, which was alarming to me as a five-year old; the solid, mostly even-tempered and predictable part of the household couldn't pick me up and hold me.

In about 1951, we got a black Austin 30. It had flickers as indicators that stuck, so it was my job to thump the side of the car from the back seat to make the flicker pop out when we were taking a corner. A holiday to Devon took many, many hours, even though we set off so early that it was dark. Mum would pack bacon and egg sandwiches. The radiator overheated easily and getting the cap off to relieve the pressure was exciting. Hissing noises followed by a volcanic eruption of rusty boiling water and lots of shouting.

Dad's parents lived miles and miles away from us in Wembley. We dutifully drove around the South Circular to see them three times a year. His father was a kind gentle man who had been a publican, running *The Admiral Duncan* in Brockley. His mother was a much sterner person, possibly due to the hand life had dealt her. Dad was the youngest and least wanted child, cared for and brought up by his siblings.

Mum regarded these family trips as an unpalatable duty and spent the journey breathing out resentment and criticizing dad's driving. The atmosphere in the car would descend from icy to revolting, reaching its nadir when we stopped to buy a gift. The worry about whether flowers could survive the rest of the journey in the poisonous air and the inevitable traffic jam around the South Circular could be relied upon to induce travel sickness every time. Near Wembley, mum and dad would point out the places where their school friends used to live or where dad and Pop had played cricket. Even a stadium where they had watched ice hockey when courting. We would be met at the front door by Auntie Bea and Auntie Joyce, dad's sisters, who lived with their parents and took care of them. Auntie Bea looked frail and her voice was querulous. Auntie Joyce was big boned and forceful. Their hair styles were so old fashioned that it must have been deliberate. Neither wore makeup and their clothes, although of good quality, were of a style that had not been in a shop in the last twenty years. I didn't understand why the sisters didn't have a house of their own. Most curtains were closed at Stapenhill Road 'to keep the light out so the furniture doesn't fade.' Odd, I thought, since you couldn't see whether it is faded or not in the half light. The sisters themselves seemed to be fading gently into obscurity. In the hall, it took time to adjust to the darkness while assessing the length of a decent interval before asking to use the toilet.

Grandma would be in bed on these visits. She and grandad had a bedroom downstairs at the back of the house that was even darker than the rest of the place. It smelt musty and faintly of disinfectant. Their double bed was enormously high. I would creep round to the side grandma was on and stand beside her, half expecting her to be dead. I'm not sure she knew who I was, so it was difficult to think of a topic of conversation in the dark. Indeed, never being able to see her properly, I wasn't entirely sure that she wasn't a wolf. I would slither out as soon as it seemed polite to do so.

The whole house was quiet and still, though not in a peaceful way, because a pervading air of resentment kept the air hopping. Dad would sit and talk to his mother but did not manage much longer than I did. He had more in common with his father, Grandad Russell, who was often outside in a wicker chair with a blanket on his knees. Grandad Russell was as jolly as Grandma Russell was dour, so dad could have a proper conversation with him. Grandad had to be helped to his feet and along the garden path as he was so frail.

I suspect the aunties' resentment was the result of Grandma Russell treating them as skivvies. Although mum did not want to spend time in the kitchen or talking to the aunties, she would offer to help to make it clear that we did not expect to be waited on. Since the aunties regarded the kitchen as their exclusive territory, mum could rely on the offer being turned down.

Later, Grandad Russell would be guided into the parlour: a small room screened from the kitchen and scullery by a heavy dark red chenille curtain. We would sit at a round table, covered with a matching dark red chenille cloth, suitable for a séance. The aunties always made us a wonderful tea; delicate salmon paste and cucumber sandwiches, home-made scones with jam and cream and home-made cakes, my favourite being Auntie Joyce's malt loaf, for which she would not give us the recipe.

During these afternoon teas, additions to the wide range of family taboos would be revealed. Questions or comments could result in stony silence if they touched on a taboo I had not previously come across, until it seemed to me that almost all subjects were taboo:-

- health, because grandma had cancer which could not be mentioned.
- work, because the family had risen above being pub landlords and did not want to be reminded of it.
- cooking, because mum hated it and the aunties were rather good at it.
- children, because Auntie Joyce had none and I was both illegitimate and adopted, neither of which could be mentioned.
- divorce, because Auntie Bea should have had one but didn't because it 'wasn't done'; her husband had been

violent, so she left him in the 1930s, taking her young daughter, with her.

- marriage, because of Auntie Joyce's illicit relationship with a married man.

My transgressions corrected, my role thereafter was to keep quiet and out of the way, so after tea, I would be allowed upstairs where there was a wind-up gramophone in a spare bedroom, atop an oak cabinet of 78rpm records. I would start with the one of Uncle Clem (dad's older brother) who had a fine baritone voice and had sung professionally. I particularly liked the words to the *Hippopotamus Song* and *Fishermen of England*. Singing was not Uncle Clem's job though. He worked at the London Water Board and smoked cigarettes all the time, which eventually killed him.

During one visit, I got Auntie Joyce on her own for long enough to ask her why she had a beautifully bound book of Burns' poems by her bed. Her bedroom was small, sparse and full of light. She explained that the poems had been given to her by someone she cared a lot about; that she read them every night before she went to sleep because she loved them so much. She described singing with the London Royal Choral Society and how beautiful it was to sing classical music with an accomplished choir. I had to change my view of her then, from someone lumpen and dissatisfied to a woman competitive enough to get what she wanted with mature taste in music and poetry, yet somewhere unfulfilled.

The journey home from Wembley would take at least two hours and when I judged the time was right, I could try out some questions from the back seat and chisel away at some of the fog surrounding the taboos. I learned that

Auntie Joyce had been given the book of Burns' poems by a Scottish man with whom she had fallen in love. He was already married and apparently no-one else would do, so Auntie Joyce stayed single. So far in my life, there had not been any explanation of, or discussion about, the institution of marriage. The rule about marriage being a permanent arrangement and the fact that divorce was shameful had to be explained to me. No-one had thought to tell me these things before. Given the aunties' life experience, I thought endless marriage a pretty stupid rule.

When I was nine, we all moved from Essex to Chislehurst in Kent. We were a determinedly middle-class family with net curtains that almost shone because mum washed them so often and rinsed them in Reckits Blue. I hated them. We had a huge stereophonic gramophone that sat in the bay window, taking up too much space in quite a small living room. Mum polished it with resentful energy. She didn't like music, objected when any of us put on a record and had made it clear that records were an unwelcome Christmas present.

We ate a family meal together in the evening, always prepared by mum, with some skill, little imagination and not much love. On a good day we managed to restrict the talk at supper to subjects that didn't upset either mum or dad. An atmosphere of tense neutrality was an achievement. On a bad day, people shouted: dad because he felt he had been slighted but, in a way, he could never quite explain or mum because this wasn't the lifestyle to which she wished to become accustomed. I found the whole environment exasperating and knowing that there had to be a better way, I made the decision in early teenage to plan my life so that I could earn my own living and make my own decisions.

Dad was a Freemason, which mum detested because he gave them money that she would have preferred to spend herself and his attendance at their meetings meant that she had to spend an evening on her own. There were many violent arguments about who decided how to spend the money dad earned, which made me wonder why dad was the breadwinner and mum stayed at home. She was just as intelligent, pushier, a social climber and ambitious. I suppose they could not step out of the roles ascribed them in those days. In my opinion, it would all have worked a lot better with mum in the rat race and dad as the homemaker.

I suspected that dad's racist views were acquired from his friends at the secret Freemasonry meetings, as they were at odds with the views of other friends and relatives. I was puzzled that dad saw nothing wrong in being overtly racist and anti-Jewish and wondered what he thought they had been fighting for in the Second World War.

On winter Saturdays, dad would listen to football on the Home Service (Radio 4). He did the football pools every week and there had to be absolute silence when the football results came on.

Although he was mostly even-tempered, dad could fly into a rage. I rarely knew what triggered these events until I caused one when I was fifteen. I grew a sweetcorn seedling for biology. It was inside a jam jar, cushioned by wet blotting paper, so that I could observe and draw the root system as it grew. Later I planted it out and it produced its own corn cobs. Dad refused to believe that this plant had started as a small seedling in a jam-jar. Heaven knows where he thought plants came from. Incredulous, I insisted, and a row blew up. He was so angry that he stormed out of the house and slammed the front door. Mum said not to worry; that he would calm down and come back. Indeed, he did come back and did apologise, but still refused to believe the origin of the corn cob. This diminished him in my eyes, simultaneously clarifying for me that he was not the all-knowing, undisputable source of knowledge I had believed him to be. I never pushed him on his beliefs again, just registered my own and left it at that. He was constantly surprised that girls and women could compete with males on an intellectual level. I think he was quite shocked that I got a place at university as this was unusual for a middle-class girl in 1964, especially one who had not been to a private school.

Chapter 4

Student, mum, doctor

I took the eleven plus when I was nine and went to grammar school. Carolyn Gruban arrived in our class in the third year in 1958. If you hadn't joined in the first year, you were essentially an outsider who struggled to make friends because the rest of us were a bit set in our ways. But Carolyn attracted friends from the start. Her inherent confidence helped, as did having two older brothers who were tall, handsome, polite and intelligent. Carolyn and I were doing the same science subjects and having been thrown together for hours in school, we became friends outside school as well.

Her parents fascinated me. Her mum was slim, elegant and calm and managed a hungry family on very little money. She had fallen in love with Carolyn's father, who was German, while he was a prisoner of war. Although the war finished in 1945, it had been difficult for him to get a job. I think he was an engineer – certainly someone who had degree level qualifications. He and one of Carolyn's brothers built a ham radio in their flat and showed me how it worked. They had taught themselves how to do this mainly from books. I was very impressed that you could learn to do something this good just by reading.

One of the brothers was also reading a paperback about the war. There were photos of people dying in a concentration camp and of mass graves. Although the war was a frequent topic of conversation amongst my parents' generation, I had not heard about the concentration camp side of things. It shocked me that there were ordinary people behaving like this in the not so distant past and not so far away. The facts were too awful to absorb, too important to deny or ignore and my brain did not want to take it in. I felt paralysed.

That teatime in Carolyn's house, we talked about the book. Her dad clearly didn't know it was in the house and questioned the suitability of World War Two concentration camps as a topic for teatime with a guest present. The subject could hardly have had more conflict potential within the family and the tension rose. Looking back, it may have been a fairly routine tussle between a teenage son who already knew everything and a kindly and intelligent father.

I took the book home and read about World War Two concentration camps on my own, in my room. The horror I felt cannot be described. I was thirteen years old and hadn't the slightest understanding that humans could be capable of such inhumanity. Had there not been photographs, I might have been able to dismiss it as fiction. But I could not. For many sleepless nights and grey days, the implications of concentration camps with their mass graves jostled with my existing world of endless unwritten rules on codes of teenage dress and behaviour. I raised the subject at home. Mum said it was best forgotten and all over with and changed the subject. Dad let out a tirade of abuse at the entire German nation.

I could not let it go. Why did the German state want to be rid of the Jews? Again, I asked my parents. Their explanation was that Jewish people closed themselves off, refused to trade with non- Jewish people and had a system of lending money only to each other. I looked again at the photos of mass graves in the book with its images of emaciated bodies of dead men, women and children. The money theory did not seem to me to explain anything.

Looking back, this was when I let go of childish things and grew up. I searched my mind for explanations. Were all people capable of treating people as the Jews were treated? Was I? The book explained that some of the people interned in concentration camps took on roles of authority, singling out others for extermination, in a bid to survive themselves. Would I have done that? Would I have done that to save other members of my family? No. Yes. No… no wonder I didn't sleep.

In an optimistic search for spiritual certainty, Carolyn and I enrolled for Church of England confirmation classes. On the evening of the first class, we heard shouting down the hall in the vicarage. The vicar, a huge red-faced man, then burst in and angrily read something from the Bible that had no apparent connection to spiritual learning. Over the weeks, this pattern repeated itself and we detected alcohol on his breath. He was a scary person in this state and his wife found it difficult to get him to take our class. We did get confirmed but the whiffs of alcohol were the only spiritual content. A couple of months later, the vicar spent the entire Sunday morning service in his pulpit in a rage about 'young people today.' Their depravity apparently knew no bounds. I felt sorry for his children. I never went back to that church.

From melted chocolate to medical school
One of my holiday jobs was at the Tip Top bakery. They started me on doughnuts. Each one had to be pushed onto a nozzle: too hard and the jam went on the floor; not hard enough and it went over me. Next, they tried me on packaging hot cross buns. The machine sealed four buns in each packet except that it wasn't set quite right and started

stamping on the edge of the buns, then on the middle of the buns, which looked really funny. I called for help.

They moved me to butter icing. This seemed relatively simple. Scoop out butter icing and sandwich together two Victoria sandwiches. Except this was the day that Marks and Spencer were coming to inspect the factory. We were given clean overalls and hats and told not to talk. The floor manager stopped to check what I was doing and said that half the sponges hadn't been frozen properly and were stale. He told me to put them in a box under the worktop. The deputy manager came along five minutes later. "What are all those cakes doing in the reject box?" he asked. I explained. "They'll have to be used. It'll affect productivity," he replied. So, for two hours, I was lifting the rejected sponges up and down according to the relative location of the manager, the deputy manager and the M&S inspector. Finally, they put me on the chocolate conveyor where we were supposed to check that each little cake had been properly covered with melted chocolate before lifting it by hand into boxes at the end of the line. Somehow, the line was either going too fast, or the machine was making the chocolate too hot. The chocolate, and then the cakes, started sticking to our hands. By the time we could attract someone's attention at the end of the conveyor, we were both up to our armpits in melted chocolate.

School remained a steadying part of my life. Our head teacher, Miss Huxstep, had a natural air of authority. You just knew, even if you didn't know the word yet, that she had integrity. I was not a brilliant student, but I was quite clever, and I worked hard. Hopeless at languages, average at Maths, and not interested in English, I was drawn to science subjects. I studied hard, got thirteen O levels and started four A level science subjects. All four required a lot of practical lessons and a timetable could not be arranged to fit everything in. For a year, I took masses of work home (formalin-soaked frogs on the kitchen table for dissection were not particularly welcome) and copied out other people's notes from classes that overlapped my subjects. For the second year of sixth form, school could not arrange a timetable for me that made sense and so I gave up Botany and just continued with Chemistry, Physics and Zoology.

My intention was to apply to medical school. This was 1962. Many medical schools required O level Latin, which I did not have of course, and many did not accept female students. It was possible to study O level Latin at my school, but I was so bad at French in my first year that I hadn't been allowed to take another language. I was allocated to domestic science instead. Medical Schools' insistence on O level Latin was justified by the fact that doctors' prescriptions were partly written in Latin, but I think it was more a system of ensuring that applicants were from a Public School.

For careers advice, I was told that if you did not have a parent who was a doctor, it was a waste of time trying to get a place to study medicine. That was enough to make me determined to get in.

At home, our parents' marriage hit rock bottom. Mum leant on me weeping. She was considering leaving dad and asked if I would leave with her. I patted her shoulder, calmed her down, and worked out a way to get dad to see the GP about his depression. I made a mental note to avoid getting myself into a marriage from which I could not afford to retreat. But it was hard to study in a home ravaged by emotional outbursts.

I applied for medical school in 1964 before there was a system for central clearing, so had to apply by hand-written letter to each of them. I was called for several interviews but had never had an interview before and my performance was mediocre, especially when confronted by snooty men asking whether my parents were doctors and which university they had been to. But justice prevailed and I was offered a place to study medicine in Sheffield, conditional on getting certain grades at A level.

I chose the crucial few months leading up to my A levels to fall in love for the first time. After six months, we broke up and this hurt my teenage brain so much that I struggled to concentrate on my revision and as a result, one of my grades was not good enough to meet Sheffield's offer. The university was kind enough to keep my place open for the following year to allow me to re-sit Chemistry for a higher grade.

During that year, between school and university, I took evening classes at Sir John Cass and Bromley High to improve my grade in Chemistry. I spent the year working at the Air Pollution Research Unit, headed by Professor Lawther at St Bartholomew's Medical School. I was a junior laboratory assistant, climbing up to the roof every morning to change the filters on the air sampling equipment. I then processed the filters so that the spectrophotometer could analyse the last twenty-four hours' sulphur dioxide, nitrogen compounds and particulates in central London air. We were part of the early warning system for smog.

I revised on commuter trains and station platforms. I kept to my revision timetable and honed my exam technique. When necessary, I even missed a Wednesday evening at ballroom dancing. In the summer, my exam result arrived by letter. I had worked so hard and it meant so much. Whoever marked my chemistry A level, whoever put the result in the envelope and flung it into the 'out' tray, could not envisage the importance of this result to me. I failed.

Despite all the work, I had worse marks than a year ago. My future dissolved in front of me. I had not seriously considered a career other than medicine since I was thirteen. I tried to adapt and accept that if I couldn't achieve a better grade with all that work, I probably did not deserve a place at university.

My teachers and my dad wanted me to challenge the result, but I felt that I had to take this blow and come to terms with it and with the prospect of having to live at home indefinitely. This was 1964. I did not know of any jobs that would pay enough to allow me to move away from home. The reality plunged me into near suicidal depression.

University of London
Senate House WC1
17th August 1964

Dear Miss Russell,

I am sorry to say that owing to a clerical error, you were misinformed about your result in Chemistry at the Advanced level, and I am glad to send you a corrected statement from which you will see that you have passed in this subject.

I am very sorry that you had this initial disappointment which I am sure will be offset by this better news. In order to avoid any confusion, will you please return the original statement of your result.

Yours very truly ……….

I did not understand why this has happened to me. I sent a telegram to Sheffield University admissions department and thankfully my place at Medical School was still available. I was infused with energy and relief. Kent County Council awarded me a grant to cover my tuition fees and most of my living expenses. In September 1964, mum drove me up the A1 to my digs in Sheffield. We could see people working on the first UK motorway, the M1. The future had begun.

Student, wife and mother

Sheffield had an enlightened approach to medical education in the 1960s. A third of students were women at a time when the custom was not to admit women to training unless they had a parent who was a doctor. For a virgin, free thinker and class warrior, the university environment was exciting, and I got pregnant at the beginning of my second year. This was 1966.

As a teenager, boyfriends were just that – friends who were boys. I didn't consider them as marriage material and was always surprised when they got 'serious' and wanted more commitment from me. My commitment was to get a degree in medicine and a career as a family doctor. Although I fell in love with some of my boyfriends, I never actively considered any of them as a life partner. And when, in the end, I became pregnant and had to get married, I still had not seriously thought about whether Ari would be a good husband or father. Not being completely impervious to social norms, I married my Greek man and became Mrs. Aristophanes Franklinos.

Our baby turned out to be a sheer delight. He gurgled and chuckled and ate and grew. My only experience of babies had been as a babysitter, so I had to learn as I went along. In his first winter, he developed a bright red rash on his face and spots that seemed to spread down his neck. Alarmed, I took him to the clinic where a pleasant nurse explained that I was 'boiling' him by wrapping him up in far too many clothes and blankets. His cot and pushchair were borrowed, and Nanna and Pop bought us a high-chair and a twin tub. I had knitted a dress for the baby while pregnant, where a jumper would have been a lot more use. This was before the days of baby-grows, so I made him sleep-suits from some sort of flannelette material that tangled up as soon as he kicked around in his cot. As he grew, people leant clothes and I was able to make him more suitable outfits. When the first Mothercare store opened in Sheffield in 1968, I yearned to buy their outfits for small boys but could not afford them.

Having my own child brought home to me how difficult it is for a mother to have her baby adopted. Having a baby changes the world. A whole new person happened. A live thing was inside me and now it is a separate live thing, which is weird and wonderful. I did not want to put either of my babies in a cot when they were small. I wanted to cradle them to be sure that they were warm and comfortable, and the rest of my life shrank to a less important shadow. When we eventually settled into the routine: feed, clean, sleep, repeat, there was space for other things. As I introduced friends and family to each new human, I marvelled at their interest in my babies, which was genuine, but not a patch on the love I felt for them. Maybe my feelings for my babies were more intense than usual because they were the only blood relatives I knew? I hated to be parted from either of them.

In 1966, it was still illegal for adopted children to search for their birth parents. I really wanted to know about my birth family but had my hands full figuring out how to look after a new baby, completing another three years at medical school and coping with hardly any money. My relationship with a new, very young husband did not offer support in those areas. So, my life was in sufficient turmoil without the challenge of starting an illegal search for my origins.

I alarmed friends, relatives and medical school principals by a sudden change in personality from placid to tigress. Nothing was going to be allowed to threaten this mother baby unit and a decent future for us depended on getting qualified as a doctor. Other students had got pregnant and left university. I was determined to continue. Fortunately, the Dean at Sheffield Medical School was sympathetic and allowed me to spend the autumn term after Alex was born going to morning lectures only.

Sheffield's undergraduate course was the first in the country to include clinical training in General Practice and to appoint a Professor of General Practice. Most medical students elsewhere in the UK were trained exclusively to become hospital doctors. Another unique part of our undergraduate course was three months' social medicine, with tutorials on epidemiology, statistics, screening programmes, and environmental health. With the Environmental Health Officer, I visited a factory that processed chickens for freezing, a small abattoir where pigs were being slaughtered and a workplace described as a sweatshop; but there had been a tip off, so it was empty and he couldn't do much about it. I sat in with a GP for his surgeries and went on home visits with him, consolidating my view that this would be my future career path. We were taken to a steel mill and I held my breath watching a steelworker walk along the rim of a vat of molten metal.

The practical sessions that I should have attended in the afternoons after Alex was born were deferred to the summer break the year after. For the rest of the students in my year, that summer break was a chance to spend eight weeks experiencing medicine in a developing country. Instead, I was down a coal mine at Orgreave.

Miners, especially Yorkshire miners, are not keen on having 'bloody students trapesing around' their underground tunnels. I should have been forewarned by the fact that fellow students who had been down the mine were guarded about it and suggested that it might be okay to miss the experience. I could not get them to explain. At the mine head, we were met by a foreman who explained the history of Orgreave mine and gave us basic safety information. There had been students in the past who had a fear of enclosed spaces, so a deep mine had not been an ideal learning environment for them. We put on boiler suits and helmets, tested the lights on the helmets and clocked in, so that someone at the pit head would know who was down there, none of which was reassuring. In fact, if the foreman had not been quite so confident and cheerful, I might have given in to my instinct for self-preservation and refused to get in the lift cage.

We walked from pithead to the cage that would take us underground. The cage had to take us down 480 yards into the earth and the only thing I knew about it was from doctors in the Orthopaedics Department. Sometimes the cable broke and miners either died or had dreadful leg injuries treated at local casualty departments. This often resulted in amputation. I held on like grim death. It was cold, dark, noisy and went down a long, long way. But nothing broke. At the bottom, we stepped over the rails for the tenders that brought the coal out and the foreman took and lit a Davy lamp. I wasn't sure whether this was routine, or he was just trying to alarm us. We followed him along the main passage, dodging tenders full of coal. Here we could stand but had to take care of jutting rocks as we walked a good distance to the seam that was being worked. Seams have names and at that time, the seams being worked at Orgreave were the Flockton and Swallow Wood seams. Our seam was only a metre high. Where we joined it, there were miners – none too pleased to see us – on their knees, hacking at the wall with pickaxes. The foreman explained that they were about to expand the seam and were creating a space for the mechanical circular saw that would run horizontally, cutting the coal out.

After some chat between the miners and the foreman that appeared none too friendly, he led us along the seam. This involved crawling on our knees over wooden sleepers, avoiding the pneumatic pit props, for about a quarter of a mile. Then he sat us in a small hollowed out alcove while he spoke rather hurriedly on his walkie talkie. He told us to crouch down, at which point the seam in front of us exploded and was brought down. The blast from the explosives was deafening and for several minutes, the black smoke made it hard to breathe. I couldn't see my hand in front of my face, and it did cross my mind that we might die. But we didn't and crawled the rest of the seam to emerge in a passageway tall enough to stand. From what I could hear of the foreman, he was very angry. It would appear that you are not supposed to collapse a seam when you know that there are people half-way along it. It is dangerous. I was proud that our group had not panicked and didn't even complain. And it gave a very useful insight into a local industry, many of whose employees would be our patients in the future.

Soup and sausages only
Until he could walk, Alex was cared for by 'Auntie Janet', a friend who lived along the road. When she was expecting her first child, I had to make other arrangements. Sheffield City Council had a network of nurseries, purpose-built during the Second World War, to enable local women to contribute to the war effort through work in the steel industry. These nurseries continued to thrive during the 1960s, as more women went out to work. Alex was at Beet Street Nursery and was always happy there. It was the best equipped and staffed nursery you can imagine, with small toilets and washbasins, tiny beds for an afternoon sleep, good food and play equipment indoors and out. He could only stay until 6pm, so I missed some late lectures.

I also had to spend time in residence at various hospitals attached to the 'on call' team for either surgery, medicine or paediatrics. Again, the medical school came to my rescue. The usual rota involved being in residence overnight for two or three days a week, but this made twenty-four-hour childcare difficult to arrange. Instead, the university reorganised my residencies so that I had all the 'on call' experience packed into three weeks. Alex spent that time with alternate sets of grandparents.

Sandwiched between attending lectures, days on the wards, revising for exams, being a parent and running the house, my marriage was neglected. To be honest, we were not ready for marriage and had no idea how to do it. I lurched through it all without thinking much, but Aristophanes carried on as though he was single. He had the chance to travel to Spitzbergen for the summer; an opportunity I would have passed on myself, but it was important to him. At the time, we were living on very little money. Single students had a smaller grant than married students, but marriage during the course of your studies did not qualify. There was no question of an overdraft being granted to someone without a job in the 1960s. Ari was studying for a degree in physiology at Sheffield, so had about three months holiday in the summer, unlike medical students who had three weeks. I assumed that he would spend his holidays in temporary work to support us. Instead he went to Spitzbergen.

Aristophanes thought nothing of asking his parents for money whenever he was short. I thought this was terrible, as his mum spoke no English and worked in sweatshop conditions, sewing fur, to support the family. His dad, who had been a journalist before they had to leave Cyprus, swept the floors at the gas works in Putney. They seemed very poor to me and despite their generosity, I felt very bad about accepting money from them.

Then, there were cultural differences, although back then I didn't know that was what they were called. I just remember a row with Ari when I served him eggs on toast for supper. He was furious. I did not know that Saturday night is the most important family meal of the week in Greek Cypriot culture, equivalent to the importance of a Sunday roast in mine. I was exasperated that he hadn't told me before. I did all the shopping and cooking and knew that we could only afford occasional meat meals, but it didn't matter to me whether they were at Sunday lunchtime or Saturday evening. It was a small thing, but exemplified assumptions we all make about how we live and who does what within a marriage. For Ari, cleaning the house and looking after Alex were also women's work. On the whole, I accepted this, but there were times when he just had to step in and do some childcare because I had to be at an evening lecture or a night on call. The end came when I discovered from friends that he had spent a whole evening at the students' union with friends, leaving Alex alone at home in his cot. He couldn't understand my fury.

And so, I ended up living as a single mum, on a single student's grant with our small son. We didn't have enough money, certainly not enough to cover the cost of both medical textbooks and food for a toddler. I got by with help from friends, by walking everywhere and eating whatever Alex left from his meal. He was entering his 'Campbells tomato soup and skinless chipolata sausages only' phase, which would not have been my first choice.

At some point in 1968, it all became too much for me and I sank into a severe depression. It was diagnosed as delayed postnatal depression. Presumably I hadn't had time to have it immediately after Alex was born. I took antidepressants for several weeks until it went away. Although the depression was the most horrible experiences that I have ever had bar none, it was also extremely useful.

In General Practice, we have a lot of patients with mental health problems and I had gained the best possible knowledge and experience for diagnosing and helping people with depressive illness. At the time, patients, especially men, were often told to 'pull themselves together.' Here is the main problem if you have depression; there is nothing to pull.

Somehow, I qualified in 1969. My ambition was still to become a GP, so I chose the jobs I thought would be most useful: three months in paediatrics, three months in general medicine and care of elderly and six months in Accident and Emergency. My first job was as a Junior House Officer at Northern General Hospital in Sheffield. We worked long shifts on call, the worst being from 8am Friday morning until 5pm Monday afternoon. Three events haunt me. A two-year old baby with Downs syndrome. He stopped breathing as his elderly parents drove to the hospital and although they ran in with him in their arms, we could not resuscitate him. They knew that he had a life-threatening heart defect but had believed that we could save him and were heartbroken. The second, a woman in her thirties in status epilepticus. She lived in residential care and had had epilepsy from birth. I was called late at night when all prescribed medications had failed to stop her fits. She was severely dehydrated. I knew that she needed a cut down to insert an IV line into her ankle. I had never seen this done but the anaesthetist on call said it was my job, not his. I called my senior registrar – never a popular move late at night - and he eventually persuaded an anaesthetist to go to the ward and put up a drip. The poor woman died the next day. I felt guilty. Third, a patient in his eighties on the geriatric ward – I don't recall why he was in hospital, but he lost consciousness in the middle of lunch. Our new registrar was assessing him when the patient went into cardiac arrest. The crash team arrived and suggested that resuscitation was not appropriate (I think because of his initial diagnosis). We stopped resuscitation efforts, but the registrar would not accept this and demanded adrenalin to inject directly into the patient's heart. This would have been some time after the patient had lost consciousness and more than ten minutes since his cardiac arrest. I tried to reason with him, but he brushed me aside and seemed distressed. Fortunately, the adrenalin did not work.

Like all junior doctors in their first job, I was a bit out of my depth, despite having done several locums as a junior doctor in my final year of study – I am not sure if that should have been allowed as I did not have medical defence insurance. There were more senior doctors that we could call for advice, but they rarely came into the hospital. I think only Obstetrics, Intensive Care and Anaesthetics had a registrar actually working in the hospital outside the hours of nine-to-five. It was routine for the junior doctors to cover for each other for short periods and on one evening, they all went off to a presentation by a pharmaceutical company – that included free food and wine – leaving me on call for 1,000 patients. My protests were to no avail. The hospital was spread out over many acres and we had a satellite phone on which the wards and switchboard operators could call us, so I was literally running that evening. Through sheer luck there was only one request for which I did not have the clinical knowledge. A patient on the renal transplant unit needed a new drip and a change of medication. The sister on duty knew exactly what needed to be done and although not allowed to do it herself, she talked me through it.

I treasure the memory of one patient, Mr. Brownlow, who I was clerking for admission one day on the medical ward. I cannot remember what was wrong with him, only that he told me about a metal plate in his head. I must have looked incredulous, so he made me feel it. Sure enough, I could feel a flat piece of metal more than five centimetres in diameter there, just under the scalp in the parietal region. He had been hit by a shell in World War One and taken to the field hospital where they thought he would die. He didn't and was shipped back home where they covered his brain with a bit of metal. Incredible. He was a cheerful, positive person because, he said, he had been on borrowed time for seventy years so what was there to worry about?

A crab sandwich too many
I moved to the Royal Hospital on West Street in Sheffield for my surgical house job as a casualty officer. There were constant power cuts, ancient noisy generators and lifts so old that you knew you would be safer on the stairs. But it was a small hospital where everyone knew everyone, and it had a friendly atmosphere. On an early shift, I was trying to take a history from a male patient, but he seemed confused and couldn't say what was wrong. Suddenly he leapt up from the examination couch and tried to strangle me. I shouted out but there were few staff around. Sister (a.k.a. the battle axe) seemed to fly in from nowhere to drag him off me. It turned out that the patient was in a fugue state after having had a grand mal fit. Sister made sure that no-one was put in that sort of danger again.

There were no motorways then and few major road traffic accidents. The worst cases we saw were usually coal miners and steel workers with work related injuries that is, apart from Friday and Saturday evenings, when the drunks hurt themselves or each other. If an ambulance was called to a serious incident and someone died, the crew had to bring the deceased to casualty for a doctor to certify death, after which they could take them to a mortuary. I was called to an ambulance one afternoon for such a task but pushed roughly out of the way by Sister as I reached the door. She spent fully fifteen minutes having a fearful row with the ambulance men. In their ambulance was a ten-year old boy who had been playing in a lift at a block of flats and had been killed with severe damage to his head. She was shouting at them, 'that young doctor has a little boy of her own. She is NOT going to see what you have just shown me. Now go.' Still muttering, they went.

Women who worked in the cutlery trade nearby often sustained minor injuries. They came in straight from work. Their work clothes included quantities of brown paper tied to their ankles and calves with string, this being the best protection from shards of steel at the time. Sometimes, when the paper was removed, there was a fall of witch hazel leaves – a herbal treatment persisting to the 1970s. Some also wore wooden clogs.

I was on call on a Saturday night. We had dealt with the drunks and the last patient had left two hours before. I had made good use of the quiet nights by learning to crochet. Half-way through a row I could hear a siren. Our hospital was opposite the Fire Station on West Street, so we wouldn't know whether the siren was for us or them for a couple more minutes. Before I had finished the row, the street doors flew open and a HUGE man on a trolley was rushed into the anaesthetic room unconscious. 'He stopped breathing in the ambulance,' they gasped. I pulled over the anaesthetic trolley and asked the ambulance men to stop chest compression while I got a tube down into the patient's lungs. I thought I must have got it wrong because I couldn't see his trachea. With a jolt I realised that this was the problem. His larynx had swollen and blocked of his windpipe. I heard myself saying, 'Carry on with compressions. I'll have to do a tracheotomy.' I had never done a tracheotomy, but I had read the book.

The nurse went to get the tracheotomy instruments, but the cupboard was locked. 'I'll call night sister for the key,' she said. I grabbed the only instrument available – a scalpel blade without a handle. The man had skin like bloody leather. I did myself serious damage but did get through and managed to intubate him that way and suck out secretions. I was shaking. The patient could then breathe on his own but was still unconscious. An anaesthetist arrived, took over his care and transferred the patient to the intensive care ward. The ambulance men and I were seriously shaken and had to be sat down and given tea. They said the man had eaten a crab sandwich. He knew that he was allergic to crab but thought he might have got over it. Anaphylaxis was not well understood in Sheffield at the time. Several colleagues congratulated me on my attempt to save him (he did not survive in the end). Some even giving me a hug, but wherever I went for the following week, there was 'don't go near her, she'll cut your throat.'

Serious maternity matters

Alex had been absorbed into his foster family for the twelve months that I had to spend living in hospital, regularly on call. He had two older foster brothers and a foster sister about his age. His foster mum, Anne, was a registered nurse and the whole arrangement worked well, apart from me literally getting heartache because I missed him so much. As my twelve months as a house officer drew to a close, I discussed with Anne the possibility of Alex staying another six months so that I could train in Obstetrics and Gynaecology and be eligible to take the Diploma. As a GP, it would be inevitable that I would have pregnant patients and safer if I had a suitable qualification. Anne agreed.

I started work as a Senior House Officer at Nether Edge Hospital in January 1974. I had to live in a flat on site in a Victorian building with an ancient switchboard. By the second week, I was sleeping so lightly that the click, when the switchboard operator plugged in a call to me, was enough to wake me. But the job that I had sought for training and experience, turned into a nightmare. The accidents and mistakes started with small issues. I examined a woman in antenatal clinic and diagnosed twins. She was in her seventh month of pregnancy and this should have been picked up earlier. Her consultant's response was to criticise and attempt to belittle me in front of her, until an Xray showed three, not two babies. The next week, with another antenatal patient, I considered that her blood pressure and swollen legs were sufficient to admit her for rest and observation. I would have to get the consultant's approval, but she flatly refused to see him 'or have him anywhere near me.' Apparently, he had diagnosed a miscarriage earlier on in the pregnancy and admitted her for a D&C (Dilation and Curettage procedure). She and her husband had been very upset by this episode, and more upset when she discovered that she was still pregnant after the D&C and did not know for sure how much harm had been done to the baby.

Soon afterwards, I was called to an emergency in labour ward where a woman had given birth to a healthy baby, the afterbirth had been delivered, but she was bleeding uncontrollably. Injections and compression were failing, and her blood pressure was falling. Our hospital was several miles from the blood transfusion service. As she began to lose consciousness, the consultant explained to her husband that the only option left to save her life, was an emergency hysterectomy. Reluctantly he agreed and she did survive. It was common for doctors who could not solve a clinical problem, to blame the patient. In this case it was clearly due to her having red hair.

The next crisis on this doomed maternity unit arose during a Caesarean section. The patient was an older mum (Mrs. S) whose labour was not progressing. The baby was becoming distressed and my senior registrar prepared her for surgery. The anaesthetist gave her a pre-med and I held her hand as we waited for theatre to be ready. She was extremely frightened, but I tried to reassure her. 'Will you make sure to look after my baby?' she asked. I thought this a bit odd but looked her in the eye and said, 'Yes of course' and we went into theatre. The anaesthetist was young and inexperienced. He administered the anaesthetic and began to intubate, as the senior registrar and I stood with scalpel and retractor at the ready. We waited and we waited. He could not get the tube down. He panicked. The patient started to turn blue. The senior registrar put down the scalpel. During a brief exchange, she had to push the anaesthetist out of the way, in order to put the face mask back on the patient and administer oxygen. She then made him take over, while she delivered the baby and completed the operation. The baby survived, but Mrs. S did not wake up. It was awful and avoidable. We learned that this anaesthetist had panicked before during an operation at another hospital and a more senior member of staff had taken over. Clearly, he should not have been working unsupervised in an isolated unit.

Mrs. S was transferred to a postnatal ward. She could no longer breathe on her own so was ventilated and had a drip up. Everyone knew. The atmosphere in the maternity unit was fraught. Senior doctors and managers from other hospitals appeared and there were raised voices. Midwives were sad and furious at the same time. Daily, they contended with the consultants on this unit behaving as autocrats rather than team members, on the understanding that these men had superior skills and knowledge. This pretence could not be sustained. How could they keep patients safe?

In addition, there were two maternal deaths during that six months when I was not involved with the cases. No-one did an independent case review. I was never asked to give evidence on what had happened, and I never heard from the Coroner. I presumed that the consultants had managed to get it all hushed up.

My senior registrar (SR) gave good advice and did what she could to restore my confidence. I had toyed with the idea of a career in Obstetrics and Gynaecology, but these events put me off the idea. As part of her encouragement, she invited me to help with the delivery of some twins. The patient was in the third stage of labour. Gowned up, I assessed her and said, 'the first one is breech.' The SR checked the breech presentation and said I should deliver the baby with her standing beside me. The baby's body emerged. We waited for the next contraction to deliver the baby's head. It would not budge. The SR took over to check. After much prodding and manoeuvring her face clouded over and she said, 'locked twins.' The midwives swiftly called in assistance, ramped up the gas and air, and collected an array of strange instruments. I had not heard the term locked twins, so did not know what was going on, but I realised that it was bad. There was a brief discussion between SR and the midwives about what to say to the patient. At this stage, they decided that it was more important to work quickly to save the baby.

Locked twins are an unusual situation that occurs when the first twin is delivered breech (bottom first) and the second twin is going to deliver head-first. If, by chance, they descend to the birth canal chin to chin, there is not space for either of them to come out, and they cannot be pushed back in. The only solution is to decapitate the first baby, push its head back inside, and deliver the second baby normally. Which is what we did. Nothing was said but everyone in the room was mortified, thinking 'poor baby.' It was bad. Explaining it to the parents was worse.

Chapter 5

Surviving Africa

In 1971, I married David and in 1973, I was pregnant again. By now, it was possible to buy ready-made clothes for your pregnancy and for your children. These were relatively expensive, so I made my own maternity wardrobe. In the later stages of this pregnancy, I became enormous and grew out of even the most generously sized outfits. Working full time as a GP, I hadn't the time or energy to make more clothes. In desperation, I went to the Mothercare store in Sheffield. I didn't believe that they would have anything big enough for me, but I was wrong. Their maternity clothes were lovely and made me feel normal again. In the flush of success, with several shopping bags attached, I floated next door to Radio Rentals. It was marginally cheaper to rent a TV than to buy one and we decided that while I was pregnant, we would upgrade from our small black and white TV to a larger colour set. The Radio Rentals salesman was very accommodating up to the point at which I asked where I should sign. 'You can't sign,' he said, 'We only accept the husband's signature.' I saw red, 'But I am paying for it.' He was unmoved. People in the queue were getting restless. I tried reason and logic but ended up spitting mad. 'If one day, you drop down in front of me with a coronary, I will step over you and fetch my husband. He isn't a doctor, but he is a man.' I stormed out.

By that evening, my rage was still close to incandescent. David had never seen me so angry, so after evening surgery, he hatched a plot. Next morning, he drove to Leeds wearing his smartest pin stripe suit with waistcoat. At the head office of Radio Rentals, wielding his furled umbrella, he explained about our problem with signing the rental agreement. They apologised and said it was company policy and produced the forms for him to sign.

He let his fountain pen hover for a moment. 'I must explain that I don't actually have an income. My wife works as a GP and gives me an allowance and I look after the children. Of course, I will try to keep up with the payments but ...' They snatched the agreement away.

Later, during evening surgery, someone from Radio Rentals arrived with an agreement. I saw him between patients. He asked me to sign.

In contrast, I had the absolute best service from the AA. Returning to my car during a snowstorm in Sheffield, I noticed a flat tyre. I put the jack in the jack point and tried to loosen the wheel bolts. Only one would move. After quite a lot of straining and jumping on the wheel wrench, I admitted defeat. I called the AA and apologised for calling regarding such a trivial matter but explained that I was thirty-seven weeks pregnant and due at evening surgery in an hour. The call handler said they had a mountain of snow-related incidents to attend to and couldn't give me a time when help might arrive. I topped up the parking meter and waited. But lo! In only fifteen minutes, the lovely AA man arrived. He did have some difficulty getting the wheel off but was sweet about it and totally restored my faith in human nature.

After JoKate was born, I carried on working full time as a GP assistant where we lived in a flat above the surgery. I enjoyed the work but as an assistant, was paid relatively little. I had applied for several jobs as a partner in practices around Sheffield, but not been successful. Finally, a vacancy came up for a single-handed practice in a poor part of the city and I applied for that. My interview at the Family Practitioner Committee (FPC) was for 2pm. I arrived at 1.45pm and was shown to a waiting room where there were two other people waiting. By 2.45pm I was getting restless and when someone from the FPC looked round the door, I asked how much longer I would be waiting as I had to collect a child from school. He looked shocked and flustered and checked my name against his list. Three minutes later, he was back with profuse apologies. He had assumed that I was the wife of one of the male applicants and that 'Dr Benson' had not turned up. The chairman of the panel apologised for the mistake. I weighed up the anger I felt against the fact that I still actually wanted the job. I accepted his apology.

I was successful and took over the practice six weeks later. It was run down and the surgery premises were due for demolition by the firm that owned the petrol station next door. We were in Darnall, a modest part of Sheffield half-way between the steel works and the nearest coal field. There was not a lot of money about and few people had a car of their own. I needed to find new premises close enough for my patients to walk to. There was nowhere suitable to rent. I had discussions with the FPC about them setting up a new Health Centre as nearly all the local practices were single-handed with dilapidated premises. The drawback was that the FPC would be the employer for all the ancillary staff: receptionists, cleaners, nurses and would make their own decisions about rental charges, appointment systems and opening hours. I had heard nothing good about the way this worked elsewhere in the city and was strongly advised by colleagues not to go down that route. I did not want an uncaring dragon for a receptionist or a mandatory appointment system, as less than half of the families on my list had a phone.

The only remaining option was to buy a terraced house half a mile away. This was 1975 and I could not get a mortgage in the general market. Fortunately, this situation had happened before, and I was able to get a mortgage from The General Practice Finance Corporation (GPFC). That was the good thing. The bad thing was that I would have to pay interest at a fixed rate of 17%.

My patients were, on the whole, lovely. The main exceptions were the shop stewards for the steel and coal unions, whose need for a sick note was consistent, month in, month out, summer or winter. I had little respect for them. The steel workers and coal miners themselves were more resilient and generally had a good sense of humour. Monday morning surgery was always very busy, sometimes with over thirty patients waiting to be seen and up to ten house calls. My nurse would get them organised, persuading some to come back later and, with my agreement, dealing with others who just wanted test results. We did consider an appointment system, but very few patients wanted it.

The practice gradually grew from a list of 1,300 patients to 2,700. There was limited back up or support apart from an excellent community midwife attached to the practice, and later, some very good GP trainees. For a while, Social Services had a presence in Darnall, but someone set fire to their offices, so that was that. The nearest hospital was two bus rides away which was just too far in terms of time, energy and cost for many patients, unless the need was dire. If I wanted someone to have a blood test done, I had to build in time to take it to the laboratory myself that day. A routine appointment for a patient to see an orthopaedic consultant on the NHS meant an eighteen-month wait. The practice nurse and I had to build up a fairly self-reliant system using common sense.

Over the first twelve months, the practice broke even financially but I could not take a salary from it. In order to pay for food and childcare, I had to work extra sessions: School Health three afternoons a week and Family Planning Clinics two evenings a week. I was on call every evening and had to employ a young local woman to 'live in' in case I had to go out on a call at night. Since I knew the patients, most calls were either so serious that an ambulance was needed or could wait until I could get there at 7am.

There was a residential care home for the elderly in Darnall, run by Sheffield Council. I had several patients there and the matron asked if I would take on any new patients who moved in, if they were too far from their previous practice. This worked well for a year or so. One day I got a call from Dr. S, a colleague, who had trained with me at Sheffield University. He wanted to visit me to have a form signed. I had liked him, but we had not met socially since we qualified. I was shocked to find that the form was for submission to the GMC to which he had been reported for illegal drug use. I examined him so that I could complete the form stating his current state of health. He said there had been a misunderstanding and wanted me to become his GP. Soon afterwards, I had a call from the husband of the matron at the residential care home. She was acting oddly, making no sense. When I saw her, it was clear that she had taken drugs of some sort. It emerged that she had become involved with Dr. S and that he was supplying her with drugs. I called him to challenge him. He mumbled down the phone, seeming similarly spaced out.

I knew of no NHS or voluntary drug services in Sheffield at that time and had no training in how to deal with this situation. I thought that perhaps I should call the police, although no provable crime had yet occurred. I called one of the senior lecturers who had taught me, and who was sensible and approachable. We devised a plan to admit Dr. S. to his ward for treatment, to which Dr. S agreed, but within twenty-four hours, had had a fresh supply of drugs delivered through the fanlight of his hospital room. When confronted, he discharged himself and disappeared. Concerned, I rang the General Medical Council (GMC). It emerged that the GMC system for monitoring a doctor with a mental health problem, was to require a report from an independent doctor every six months. The independent doctor was chosen by the doctor who was being monitored and could be a different person every time. Nothing I told them would be regarded as admissible evidence. I suggested that this was not a very clever system, allowing indefinite delay for a drug addicted doctor to be diagnosed, offered treatment or struck off. I tried several times but was met with a 'there there, little woman' type response from elderly men at the GMC. Incensed, I wrote to the president, explaining that I felt that I had a public duty to ensure that action was taken to prevent an active drug user from practicing medicine. If they would not act, I would report this to the police and then to the papers. Whether or not this influenced them, I do not know, but they acted soon afterwards.

Searching for my birth parents

The Houghton Committee reported to the government on the issue of allowing adopted children access to their birth records in 1972 and there was national debate on the subject. I could not avoid hearing coverage of how women had been coerced into giving their babies for adoption, which enraged me. When JoKate was born in 1973, my interest in finding my birth mother resurfaced. I also had to think about the fact that finding my birth mother wasn't just about me because I now had children who did not know their natural grandparents.

The law changed in 1975 with the Adoption Act and it became legal for me to search for my birth parents. My adoptive parents were living in Kent and although they had always been reluctant to discuss anything to do with my adoption, they had told me my original name and where I was christened. I did not know anyone else in my situation and had no-one to discuss things with. Should I start a search on my own without my adoptive parents' knowledge? It felt deceitful after all they had done for me and saved me from.

In the end, I plucked up courage to visit Somerset House and look for more information. This was 1977, before the IRA bombings, and there was little security. I didn't have to check in. On a dreary, rainy afternoon in London, not knowing quite how to do this, I walked past a man in uniform who looked like a retired policeman. He was standing by the door looking official. That was it. That was the security. I found the enormous ledgers containing registrations of births entered by hand in chronological order. The system was that you trawled through them to find the record of birth in the ledger for that year, which provided a code number from which you could then request a copy of the birth certificate. I was searching for my birth certificate and for that of my birth mother. Since it had been illegal until recently, I was feeling rather guilty. It was also an unusual act of rebellion on my part which felt very scary.

I had been told that my mother was very young when I was born and assumed that this meant she was about eighteen years old. Despite having an unusual surname, I found no record of her birth for that year (1928) or the two years on either side. And so, I searched for the entry for my own birth, but strangely it was not in either the regular ledger or the adoption ledger in either my birth name or my adopted name. I ran out of time and slammed the ledgers shut in a fit of rage. How dare they suggest that I did not exist? The official system for obtaining adoption files required me to apply to have a social worker in Sheffield and become a case, so that she could apply on my behalf for my adoption files. I had one interview at Sheffield Social Services but did not hear any more.

Lagos calling

By now (1977), David's job with ICL had moved to the firm's London head office. He used to lay his suit, tie and shirt neatly on the bannisters on the landing where he could dress without disturbing me on Monday morning, then leave for the 7am Master Cutler from Sheffield to London. One day, I found out by accident that he had spent the night with someone else. He said that it was a one-night stand and he was sorry. He seemed as sorry about being found out as about the infidelity. The next week, I started checking. I called the hotel he said he would be staying at. They had no record of him. I checked the credit card statement on his desk. There was no entry for an hotel, but one or two for theatres, building suppliers and furniture sales in London. I confronted him, but he refused to talk about it. In a fury, I attacked the clothes he had laid out for travel to London the following morning. I cut the buttons off the suit, then cut his tie in half and cut the sleeves off his shirts. His initial reaction was to suggest that I was mentally ill and needed help but did gradually realise how angry I was and that something had to be done. His solution was to accept a job with ICL in Nigeria as country manager. I agreed to go with him. I now know that neither of these statements makes sense.

We threw a leaving party for over a hundred friends and realised we had no logical explanation for why we were leaving Sheffield for Nigeria. David travelled to Lagos in October 1977 to give him time for a handover from Reg, the previous ICL country manager. While he was there, he placed an order for a new company Mercedes, as you do. He liked big cars. I once asked why, and he said it was because they were safer on the motorway. The children and I used to travel on the motorway in my Renault 4. Apparently, that was safe enough for us. I gave three months' notice, resigning from the General Practice I had built up in Sheffield. There was much to do if we were to make an orderly exit. I arranged the family's vaccinations, immunisations and paludrine to prevent malaria. Even the cats had to have jabs – because they were coming with us.

We would be taking over the house on Ikoyi, currently rented by the Reg and his wife. There was a good primary school within walking distance for JoKate. Alex was eleven and we were advised against sending him to the only secondary school in Lagos for expats because it was alleged that there was a serious problem with drugs amongst pupils there. This alarmed me as it was not a common problem in Sheffield in the 1970s, as far as I knew. I opted for him to stay in the UK for schooling instead. Having no personal experience of boarding schools, I embarked on a tour of the ones that were recommended and that we could just about afford. From these, we chose Uppingham. Alex would have to pass Common Entrance in order to gain entry and so he had to go to a 'crammer' for a year to achieve this. I felt out of my depth with these decisions.

We decided to rent out our home in Sheffield for the duration of David's two-year contract in Nigeria. It was a huge Victorian house, but we had put a lot of time, money and effort into making everything work. When we first saw it, I loved it, but insisted that the solid fuel boiler in the kitchen – a Stove Esse - would have to go. It was far too old fashioned. In our first six months, we ripped out rotten floorboards, replaced sash window weights, rewired, put in central heating (two separate Servowarm systems because there wasn't a domestic system with a pump that would cope with circulating water on three Victorian sized floors) and replaced the lead pipes for the water supply. There were whole weeks when our only source of heat, hot water and an oven was the Stove Esse in the kitchen. I insisted that we keep it.

Like most old houses in Sheffield, ours had suffered subsidence, the ground beneath us all being a lattice of coal mines. When disused, the tunnels often collapse and the ground settles. This was particularly noticeable in the front room, where the architrave had fractured and slipped a good six inches on one side. It alarmed our surveyor, but we decided we could live with the risk and got a mortgage. We stopped noticing the subsidence until I chose some wallpaper for that room. This had large orange squares. If the squares looked straight where they met the mantelpiece, they definitely did not where they met the ceiling. We decided not to look at the ceiling.

The house was built in 1840 from local stone, giant blocks of it. Over the years, the exhaust from the chimneys at the steelworks had blackened the stone, so we arranged for it to be sandblasted clean. I was in the middle of morning surgery one day when I had an urgent call from Julia, JoKate's nanny. 'There's a spaceman at the window. He's got a gun.' Sure enough, there was a man in a space suit hauling a huge pressurised hose up a ladder aiming at our stonework. We had forgotten to tell her about the sand blasting.

By the time we were ready to leave for Nigeria, the house didn't need much attention to be ready to let, except that I had had a couple of bites on my legs that looked suspiciously like flea bites. The council arranged for treatment and the van duly arrived, clearly labelled 'pest control,' at the very moment our first prospective tenants turned up. What can you say?

David returned to help finalise arrangements for letting the house and we all flew to Nigeria on 5th December 1978. Dad said, 'Look up Akintola Williams. We were accountants together at Binder Hamlyn twenty-five years ago.' Righto dad. Nigeria is only six times the size of England. Mum was certain that we would all be murdered in our beds. In fact, my main struggle would be with day to day things like the lack of phones or postal system, intermittent supplies of water and electricity, and how to work a generator. I did not have a car or driving licence and the shops were miles away. I had never had servants before, and I had to get JoKate enrolled in her first school.

Expat life begins

Our first visitor was the fish man. He arrived with a wooden box on the back of his push bike, filled with fresh fish and a lump of ice. I didn't recognise any of the fish, although this may have been because I mostly bought fish fingers in England, Sheffield being as far from the sea as you could get. I bought the ones he called 'sole' as they sounded promising.

With help from other expats, things came together and in January 1978, I flew back to the UK to take Alex to his new school. Back in Lagos, we went to the Ikoyi Club one evening. A lot of expatriates were members there, but I wondered why there were so few women at the bar. Was I committing a social gaffe by being there? I was reassured that women were welcome but slightly alarmed to hear that most of the wives had chosen to stay in Europe. Did they know something that I didn't?

The daily lives of expatriate women in Lagos seemed strange to me. Some, especially middle-aged women married to men from the British High Commission, did not seem interested in Nigeria. Their daily routine would have been very similar in Surrey. They played bridge most mornings, did not mix much with the rest of us and had much of their food flown in by the Foreign Office so that they did not have to cope with the shortages affecting the rest of us. Their conversation was mostly about what was happening in the UK and how awful Nigeria had become since independence. We enjoyed cornering them when they were tipsy and getting them to point out which of the men at the High Commission were spies. Another group seemed to drink quite a lot of gin and wear quite a lot of makeup. I gravitated towards the third set (mostly American) who had the refreshing 'can do' attitude of frontierswomen. They invited me to help at a local hospital (no electricity, no bed linen) and visit the market with them. In the market, there were said to be stalls that sold herbs and dead babies for traditional healers. We avoided those and focussed on locally produced vegetables and crafts.

The frontierswomen gave me sensible advice. There were frequent military coups, so be prepared, don't go out when there is gunfire and always have a week's worth of fresh water and dried food in the house. Register as a resident with the British High Commission and let them know the dates when you are out of the country and don't react if you get racist abuse when you are out shopping. In fact, I never did get any abuse. We were sometimes called Oyinbo, the Yoruba word for peeled banana, but this seemed to me to be an attempt to classify the tribe we were from. It was extraordinary to most Nigerians that we could not supply a tribal name when asked. At first, I found this amusing, but on reflection, began to wonder why I didn't know my tribe. How far back in history was my tribal identity obliterated? Tribal identity was still strong in Lagos and people had a common understanding of how to behave both as an individual and their role within their tribe. It seemed so natural, but then I supposed it could have been stultifying too. I would probably have had to break out, and maybe it would have been even harder than choosing university instead of marriage when I was a teenager in the UK.

David's new company car (a Mercedes) arrived. It had air conditioning that worked. David had a driver paid for by the company as did most expats. There had been a spate of people faking accidents and accusing a white driver of running them down. The white driver was then thrown in jail until a suitable amount of compensation had been paid. It was cheaper to employ a driver. I drove myself to the beach one day to watch the local fishermen land their catch. When I turned to pick up my shoes with the car keys attached, they were gone. A man was running up the beach with them. I called, 'Stop thief' and ran towards him, at which point, three other men in long white kaftans converged to block me from the thief. I stopped shouting. The car was gone, of course, and I walked home barefoot and terrified.

Within a month of arriving, I went down with flu. It was a really bad bout and David was away in Kaduna on business. On Sunday afternoon, I passed out on the sofa. Three hours later I was shaken awake by a concerned neighbour. 'I've given your daughter her tea,' she said, testily. I tried to get up and apologise at the same time, but it was too much for me and I collapsed again. Thus, began my friendship with Blanche, who had been in Lagos for some time and knew how things worked. She was a nurse and diagnosed my malaria on the spot, despite my protestations that I had not missed any tablets. She and Harvey lived across the road and had found JoKate at their gate after lunch chatting to their daughter. When she asked JoKate where her parents were ('Daddy's gone away, and mummy is lying down') she assumed that I was 'lying down' due to gin. She gave me a loading dose of nivaquine and put me to bed. Next morning, she collected JoKate for school and then took me to a doctor. Who knows what would have happened if Blanche hadn't been there?

I planned to be a stay-at-home mum in Lagos for the first time, at least until the children had settled into their new schools. I missed Alex so much that it hurt and although I am not a worrier by nature, did not adapt well to being unable even to at least speak to him on the phone every week. His father was on a prolonged trip to India, but friends and family rallied round to make sure Alex had somewhere to go at half term.

JoKate on the other hand, did settle straight into Lagos life. Her school, St. Saviours, was very good. She joined Brownies and learnt to swim and dive between numerous social engagements.

In March 1979, Yinka Gbajumo came to call. He was a UK educated Nigerian doctor and asked if I would work with him as a GP in Lagos. I explained that I had no training in tropical medicine, but this didn't seem to matter. I had my qualifications and he would sort out registration with the Nigerian Medical Council and provide a car. He also offered a good salary. I accepted.

Expat men fell into parallel groups with the expat women. One group just worked and drank. Another group did some work and held cocktail parties. They bemoaned the passing of Empire and frequented the Motorboat Club. The third group, mostly younger, worked and worked then met at the Sailing Club. There was friendly rivalry between the boat club and the sailing club and people from both entertained us generously when we arrived in Lagos, but the discordant bagpipes of the Nigeria Black Watch at the boat Club on our first Burns Night were too much for me. How did these people keep their faces straight? We joined the sailing Club instead and bought a Shearwater but stayed friends with many boat club people because they were nice, and you need access to a motorboat for water skiing.

Sailing in Lagos harbour was not for the faint hearted and a fearsome place to learn. David was skipper and I was crew. This, apparently, legitimated him swearing at me. Launching our wooden catamaran was difficult, as you were straight from the slipway to a tidal race at most states of tide. It was advisable to have your sails hauled-in ready to catch whatever wind there might be and get going swiftly, as ocean going cargo ships were in and out all the time, and they took your wind. It was exciting until the day we tried getting back onto the slipway and missed the slot. We came alongside long enough for JoKate and me to be pulled off, but David and the Shearwater drifted towards Falomo bridge. David took a line from the club motorboat, but the current was too strong, and he and the Shearwater were washed away by a flooding tide. I watched in horror as the boat was dashed against the bridge, turned over and disappeared under water.

The Shearwater was no more. The yard, where we stored our sailing boats, was by now full of yacht club members shouting for rescue vessels, fending off other boats that were trying to come into land or trying to console me. It took twenty minutes for David to be found and brought back from under the bridge in the rescue boat, by which time I was shaking with fear, certain he had drowned.

Alex flew out to be with us for the four weeks of the Easter holidays. By now, I knew people with children his age and social activities were new and exciting for him. He went to parties, the pool and the museum. He tried water skiing and squash. We all dressed up for an Ugly Bug Ball, and he competed with Blanche and Harvey's older daughter making the best peppermint creams. He was very unhappy about going back to school, but I could not think of a practical alternative.

My work routine could be challenging, alarming, but never boring. I remembered dad's note and asked Yinka whether he had heard of someone called Akintola Williams. Sure enough, he had, and I tracked down Akintola's office. He wasn't there but I left a note and was delighted when we were invited to his house for lunch. I say house. It would have been closer to describe it as a palace. Lagos was an amazing place.

With the Shearwater sunk and destroyed, we decided to buy another boat. This time a Hobie 16, which we shared with Roger. It was a catamaran, like the Shearwater, but made of fibreglass so more resilient. It had rainbow coloured sails called Tequila Sunrise and went like shit off a shovel. Crewing on this was even more exhilarating. David and Roger both became expert skippers at making it go very fast. As crew, I would be wearing a harness and hooked onto a line attached to the mast so that I could lean out over the water and balance the boat. Then we could go even faster. David and Roger were less expert at preventing pitchpoling, when the prow dug into a wave, the boat came to a sudden stop then went head over heels. When the boat stopped like this, the skipper could hang onto the rudder and trampoline then slide gently into the water. The crew, however, was hooked on and hanging out on a wire. Having nothing to hold onto, she was thus carried in a forward direction at speed and came into close contact with metal stays and the mast, sustaining multiple contusions before sinking into the filthy water of Lagos harbour, frantically trying to release her harness. There would be no time to express any views on this as the skipper would be yelling instructions about swimming to the mast head so that the boat could be righted, and we could sail off without losing our place in the race.

In August, we took annual leave and flew to California with JoKate and Alex. We went to Disneyworld and Marineworld and fell in love with San Francisco. I also managed to gain four kilos in a week, which I put down to a new and insatiable appetite for fresh orange juice. From California, we flew back to the UK for the rest of our leave, visiting friends and family.

New Year's Eve 1979 was our second in Lagos. We had tickets for the yacht club dinner and dance but failed to notice until the morning of the event that dress was 'Red Sea Rig.' We had no idea what this meant, and spent the day asking around. No-one else seemed to know either but were guessing that it meant dressing like shipwrecked mariners. I had the day off, but we were chased by a motorboat on our way to the beach and I had to get off our Hobie to minister to a sixty-year-old Englishman with a fever who had also had two epileptic fits. He has been in the bush for three months and was waiting for a plane home. His wife was understandably distraught and couldn't explain why he had a supply of heart tablets. The patient looked pretty ill to me and was slightly confused. I discovered nothing to explain his condition on examination, so took a blood sample. It would have to wait for analysis tomorrow as the labs were all closed. I gave him intramuscular chloroquine as common things occur commonly and I couldn't rule our cerebral malaria. With instruction to keep him cool and hydrated, I returned to the children and the beach, telling his wife to fetch me if he lost consciousness.

On Atlas beach, Alex and JoKate greeted me as though I had been gone for a year. Alex was being taught to water ski by half a dozen people who could not water ski themselves. He did manage to hang on long enough to get out of the water but was skiing very fast in a crouching position. In the middle of the busiest shipping lane in West Africa, he fell off. I could see an ocean freighter approaching a quarter of a mile away, so was hugely relieved when the motorboat circled and picked him up.

I helped JoKate dig canals in the sand when thousands of dragonflies swarmed over us. Fascinating for a few minutes, then a bit threatening, but soon they were gone, who knows where. Back at home, I gave the children their tea and had a shower before the friends of the sick Englishmen arrived with a progress report. We had the usual dilemma of whether to risk admitting him to a Nigerian hospital or try to get British Caledonian to fly him out quickly. I visited him again but by then his company doctor had been located so I was absolved from further clinical decisions.

I joined David at the yacht club where it turned out that Red Sea Rig was full dinner dress, but the men did not have to wear jackets. After the meal, David and Alex got into a beer fight with someone on the balcony. Alex, having less skill in this matter due to being only thirteen and having his first beer fight, allowed some of his beer to besmirch the dress of the lovely Lady Helen, who threatened him with court action for damages and a new silk dress. David rescued him. Alex was the hero of the night with the blokes after that and was grandstanded repeating what the Lady Helen had said in her plummy accent.

I was ignorant of all this and sober due to the possibility of being called upon again to treat the Englishman with a fever. I was also slightly distressed that Roger still wasn't there when the meal finished. He rolled up at ten o'clock with Pepsi in tow (flash bird). Of course, he had a perfect right to bring her and dance with her like that, but I could not resist the urge to land a hard kick on his arse that knocked them over. Discerning friends dragged me away to dance. At midnight, we sang *Auld Lang Syne* and cheered Margaret George, who really is Scottish and wore a kilt. She and five friends took the first sail of 1980 alongside the yacht club in the dark.

So began the worst of bad years. No day would be complete without being woken by a power cut after two hours' sleep, followed by generators starting up in all the surrounding houses. One night, I rose to have a wee and wash my hands and a HUGE cockroach flew out of the sink into my face. I missed England. We were invited to the Ritters' for drinks at lunchtime. There was nothing for the children to do and the Ritters' huge dalmatian dog was breathing on the finger food. Someone fell over drunk and we left. I missed England a lot. Our Nigerian landlord demanded a hugely increased rent to be paid offshore in Sterling and it was unlikely that David's company would pay for this, so we faced having to move. JoKate had stomach pains and wouldn't eat. I kept examining her but couldn't diagnose the problem. I was worried. Alex hated his school. There were tears, pleas and heart-rending scenes but I still couldn't work out an alternative that was practical for us all and would give him a good education. I hung onto the hope that he would pass his Common Entrance exam this term and get a place at Uppingham where I hoped he would be happier. Besides, I had to be back at work on 3rd January.

By now, I had a front door key for Roger's house. I dropped by one morning in early January to remonstrate with him about the Pepsi incident at the yacht club, only to find them in bed together. I returned the key. We did, however, continue to sail our Hobie 16 with Roger as skipper and myself as crew. Despite a fairly poor result from our race on the fifth of January, we stayed to watch a film on Hobie sailing in USA. They showed Hobie 14s coming onto the beach so fast that they glided straight over the sand bar and into the lake beyond. Impressive. And there was a Hobie 18 going so fast, that someone could water ski behind it. We never get that much wind in Lagos.

At the surgery, there was the usual parade of people complaining of 'general weakness of the body' and 'tired all the time.' Some expats had dreadful laryngitis with swollen throats and high temperatures. The old coasters had taken the edge off it with penicillin scrounged from friends. People newer to Lagos had hung on until surgery reopened. Honestly, I used to complain about home visits in the UK but one or two of them were really too ill to be out. I gave some of the worst affected a triplopen injection to speed recovery but had to limit it as my stock was low and the Israeli alternative that we got in Lagos hadn't been stored safely.

At the surgery, all the antenatal checks were booked with me. Many expat women wanted me to falsify their expected date of delivery to enable them to fly home when they were thirty-eight weeks pregnant (the airline wouldn't take them if they were over thirty-four weeks). An equal number wanted me to say that they should leave as soon as their pregnancy was confirmed, leaving their husbands to sweat out the dry season alone. I could understand that.

January brought a few patients with machete wounds which was, apparently, normal for the time of year. Nigerians were very keen to get hold of stereo equipment and TVs for the black market, so expats employed night watches to deter them. Roger was burgled and his night watch disappeared, but the police found him and locked him up. His 'brothers' kept turning up at the house asking Roger to get him released.

The Hausa night watches tend to stay and fight, even if outnumbered. Stitching them up was a strange experience. They regarded wounds sustained in the line of duty as inevitable and to be borne without comment. A friend had to accompany them to surgery to explain the incident because talking about it themselves would have diminished their honour. An honourably sustained wound conferred a state of grace, and the Hausa became detached and distant. In this state, he did not feel pain or care if the wound was fatal. It was for his comrades to see that he got treatment and make all the arrangements. The patient would not even discuss whether or not he should have a local anaesthetic. I talked to the friend about this, but he didn't know either, so I proceed without anaesthetic. The Hausa was conscious and looked straight forward but did not flinch or move when I stitched up his wound and administered a tetanus injection and penicillin.

Rounding the mark correctly

JoKate was seven on 10th January 1980, so we had a party. She seemed well again, which was a relief. She had a long dress and her friends brought presents. Pass the parcel was a great success and had to be played four times before the birthday tea. The jelly did not set, we ran out of ice cream and the children did not like the meringues I had made. Back to pass the parcel, but the power went off so there was no music. Instead, I let them run around the house creating mayhem, then sat them down and told them a story until parents arrived at 6.30pm.

I could not get through to Alex on the phone for most of January. It was difficult to get a line for an international call and sometimes, when I did, the master at Alex's prep school would not let me speak to him because he had strict rules about when his pupils could talk to their parents. I collapsed crying after every failure.

After Roger and I raced the Hobie one Saturday, Brian raised a protest about whose boat rounded the mark correctly. A formidable protest committee was formed and called on crew members to give evidence. I explained what happened. They then asked me what my skipper said to the other skipper. I blushed and left. We won the protest, which was good because the other skipper was a bully and quite horrid. His crew, Stuart, who was leaving Lagos soon and embarrassed about the protest, agreed to let me inherit his catering pack of Marmite. So, victory was mine. At Stuart's leaving do, there was much beer throwing. The bar steward, John Onuoha, had to ask with each order whether the beer was for drinking or throwing as he kept the drinking beer cold and the throwing beer warm.

I was invited to write a short article for the yacht club newsletter about the health hazards of sailing. I included a warning about stepping in the stream of overflow from the drains when launching, how to set broken toes, and the mental and physical health hazards of crewing. They included the photo of me turning up to crew for George, covered in bruises from the week before (George does not see fit to warn crew when he is changing tack) wearing a crash helmet and Alex's skateboarding knee protectors and elbow pads. George was furious but had no other crew so had to put up with me. Everyone else thought it was funny.

David's boss arrived from England towards the end of January and I realised that my only topics of conversation were worrying about Alex and JoKate and the difficulties at work. Roger phoned to say he was in the UK and was making arrangements to sail in the Antigua Race Week at Easter. Would I like to accompany him? David said, 'Go for it,' so I said yes. David wanted us to have separate holidays that year, his being skiing in February. We had never had separate holidays before. I was not sure about it. I seemed to love both of them and when Roger returned from annual leave, he and David teased me about it. I was not comfortable with this and our ménage-a-trois was fuelling gossip. We spent a lot of time together sailing, watching films at the yacht club, drinking at the bar.

The violence increases
In early February, David flew to Switzerland for his half of the 'separate holidays' agreement. People came around to play Acquire and Roger just seemed to stay the night afterwards. He said that he loved me. It had been a while since anyone I cared about said that.

JoKate seemed ill again, so I didn't go out much while David was away apart from going to work. Roger took to sitting at home with me and playing scrabble, which was unlike him. He was a party animal normally. After a week, I began to wonder when he would tire of it and start staying out at night. In fact, I half wished he would, as I could more easily nurse a broken heart at this stage than end the affair myself. If I had thought David was skiing unaccompanied, I would have felt guilty and tried to have the 'Let's be sensible,' talk with Durman. But I knew David was with that Maggie bird from Personnel at head office and it made me feel rather forlorn.

Three days later, JoKate was much better and I finally got to speak to Alex in the UK. He was not any happier but being brave about it. His Common Entrance Exam was on 25th February and he would be back in Lagos by 11th March, thank goodness.

David returned from skiing on the twentieth of February and I wasn't particularly pleased to see him, which was disturbing. He didn't give the impression of having missed me much either. Better not to think about that. Roger called round within the hour, which was not very discreet of him, but he said he couldn't stay away. Life got back to normal. Work, letters to Alex, JoKate not ill, but not quite well either. David, Roger and I went everywhere together as before. It was beginning to seem un-natural. Should I have suggested that he move in and we all live together? Why did neither of them want to talk about this? Roger was very upset by David's ski holiday photos. Apparently, the set I was shown had all the Maggie shots removed, but bigmouth Benson could not resist boasting of her to Roger, who was angry that I was being two-timed. After what we had been doing! Men!

David had only been back from holiday for a week when he said he had to go to London for a conference on 4th March. I suggested that JoKate and I go with him so that I could get a consultant opinion on why she has these stomach pains and then we could all fly back with Alex on 11th March. David grunted, which was a 'no.' I guessed that we did not fit into his London scene.

On the second of March, we were woken by someone throwing stones at the window. David unlocked the security gate and went downstairs then came rushing back to explain that thieves had entered the flats where many of his ICL expat staff lived on Victoria Island. Mary, one of the people living there, had been terrified and was now in danger of losing her baby. We roused our own steward to take care of JoKate if she woke and drove to the flats. The thieves had gained access to each of the flats through a service entrance and held the occupants hostage by threatening them with machetes, while their accomplice searched the flat for money and goods. It took time for them to be satisfied that the amount of cash handed over was all they were going to get, but during that time they terrified the children and their parents so much that Mary began to miscarry. The police were informed but no charges were brought. One UK staff member had only been in Lagos for a week. He left by the first plane out.

The next week brought more violence. One bedtime, an unconscious child was brought to our door. She had had malaria and had been treated by the witch doctor. Few people in Lagos could afford western medicine. Her treatment consisted of the application of cow urine to the soles of her feet, which were now blistered. I gave her a suitable injection and they took her to a hospital where she could be given intravenous medication. Next day, a woman was carried into my waiting room at the end of evening surgery. She had been in labour for more than twenty-four hours. I examined her but did not have the skills or equipment to help. Somehow funding was arranged for her to be treated at a local hospital. A very deformed baby was delivered by Caesarean section, but both baby and mother died.

I felt traumatised and tried to carry on as usual because that was what the expats in Lagos did. Unless they were part of the British High Commission, in which case they just got on a plane and went home. As David and I prepared to go out for supper with friends one Friday evening, I had to call David from his shower to speak to a colleague from the office. Tom was missing. Tom was David's most senior UK trained computer engineer. He had flown to Kano four days earlier to effect repairs on a state mainframe. They had just got through to ask why he had not arrived. We never knew for sure what happened but did learn that there had been a crash involving taxis from the airport and a petrol tanker at about that time. There were no survivors or identifiable remains.

Tom's disappearance was bad enough, but within days, the man appointed to replace him became ill. He was not my patient, but David discussed his case with me because despite hospital investigations, they couldn't find anything wrong with him. He became weaker and weaker to the point at which his life seemed in danger. People in the office were convinced that someone had put a spell on him. They alleged that relatives of Tom believed that his replacement had precipitated the car accident that killed him – again through the actions of a local medicine man. We were told that the only way out was to find the person who made the spell and buy it back. Of course, we thought the whole idea ridiculous, but in conversation with old hands who had been in Nigeria for many years, we were persuaded that this was, in fact possible. David bought the man's life back. Confused, I tried every avenue to prove to myself that this was just a trick to extort money, but the more I learnt about native medicine, the more respect I had for its power. I remembered Yinka, when I started work, saying that I should always ask local people what native medicine they were already taking for their condition before I prescribed because of the danger of interactions. His reasoning was that native medicine was ineffective. But if so, how could there be interactions?

By now, I was jumpy, shaking, unable to sleep and generally feeling unsafe. Unusually, David said he would look after JoKate while I sailed the Saturday race with Roger. Half-way through the race, a speedboat came alongside and took me off to treat a seriously ill patient. At this time, I was the only white doctor in Lagos and thought to be the safest bet in an emergency. The guy was ill with a chest infection. With no access to Xray facilities on a weekend, his options were to wait until Monday, take a car to LUTH (Lagos University Teaching Hospital that was quite a distance away) or fly home. He flew home and was diagnosed with pulmonary TB (tuberculosis). Many Scandinavians arrived in Lagos with all the necessary preventive medicine for cholera, typhoid, yellow fever and malaria, but no protection against TB. The final straw for my nerves came the night before David was due to leave on

4th March. There was an enormous car crash on the dual carriageway near our house. All the lights went out and there was screaming. I am usually calm in a crisis, clear thinking during a medical emergency and keen to help whenever I can. I grabbed my stethoscope and rushed to the front door. There I froze. This was Nigeria. There would not be an ambulance, fire engine or police car. My nerves were in shreds after all that had happened and for the first time, I failed. I had become so frightened by life, that I could not go and help.

Time to leave

David refused to delay his planned trip to London even though there was some concern that other ICL properties might be targeted by the robbers who had attacked the ICL flats on Victoria Island. Rather than leave JoKate and me unprotected, he asked Roger to come and stay while he was away. David had never been particularly caring, and now showed that he was, in fact, indifferent. He had always preferred the life of a bachelor and when challenged, he would turn violent. I had always blamed myself and believed that if I loved him enough, he would change. There was a huge contrast in my time with Roger. I could relax for a week at a time without fear of attack. I could see how unhealthy my marriage had become.

Back in Lagos, David told me that he had renewed his contract with ICL to work in Nigeria for another two years. He had not consulted me. I told him that I would be leaving. Two years away from practice in the UK meant that I needed to catch up with professional development. Four years would be too much; my standard of clinical practice in Nigeria was, of necessity, lower than in the UK. There was less opportunity to investigate patients and so diagnosis was more often by guess. This can become a bad habit. David was furious. There was no discussion, just another beating. As I fell to the floor, he shouted at JoKate to go to her room. Udo, the cook, emerged from the kitchen but was sent away. Blows rained down on me. I tried not to scream because I didn't want JoKate to come in and see this. I fought back, but David started kicking me and I fell again. This was our last battle and my refusal to fight infuriated him. I got to the point at which I thought I would die. He briefly came to his senses and I crawled out of the room to get JoKate. But he was there at the bottom of the stairs coming towards me again with fists. So, I had to leave.

At Roger's house, I crawled onto the sofa and checked my wounds. I didn't think I had anything broken but something had happened to my back. I could not straighten it. Roger came home. He asked how I got the bruises on my face, then saw more on my legs and arms. It took three weeks for the bruises on my back to come out. David did call round to apologise. I wouldn't talk to him. There was a risk of a fight between the two alpha males, but fortunately Roger restrained himself. The next morning, I couldn't get to work, but took a taxi to see Blanche. She tried to get David to see sense and let JoKate go but failed. Instead, we set up a system of close watch amongst all the women we knew so that we could intervene if JoKate didn't turn up for school. Someone checked with her every day to ascertain whether she was frightened, and we planned that they would snatch her away if there was any sign of violence.

I kept a low profile and was reassured that I retained the friendship of almost all my women friends. The expat community was small, and we had given them plenty of gossip material, but marriage breakdown happened every week. Not for nothing was Lagos regarded as a punishment posting. Gradually things settled and we began to share parenting, especially when David went away on trips up country or back to the UK. We had always had separate bank accounts, so during one of those trips I went through his papers to see how things stood. David had run up debts with credit cards that more or less balanced the amount in the bank, but he was still paying the UK mortgage. He was also still seeing someone in the UK and had started a new relationship in Nigeria. You had to admire the man's libido.

Alex flew out for the Easter holidays and stayed at Roger's house with us. He tried driving my car, a two stroke Daihatsu – straight into Roger's front hedge. Roger gave him a guitar and Alex spent the summer learning to love it and meeting up with other boys his age who were there for the holidays. Alex and Jo loved the rainy season, paddling along roads and finding coloured fish in the storm drains. There were the usual picnics on the beach, water skiing lessons and expeditions up the creek. Alex had passed his Common Entrance exam and been accepted to start at Uppingham in September. He still wasn't happy. 'Give it a term,' I said.

We had just got home from playing squash after work when there was frantic banging. Roger's front door flew open before we could reach it and Phil was carried in covered in blood. He had been stopped in his car at gunpoint up the road. In a panic, he had tried to reverse the car and had been shot through the window. The car had been stolen and someone brought him to me. The bullet had gone through his neck, grazing a piece off his jawbone and taking off the top of his tongue. When he breathed out there was a faint whistle from the exit wound. He was in shock. We moved him to the back room where there was a bed and I examined him as best I could. The bullet seemed to have missed his spinal cord and all major arteries and veins. The wound on his tongue was beginning to clot and he was breathing. His blood pressure was okay, but I didn't know for how long. I gave him IV fluid replacement. I offered painkillers but he said he didn't need any. After that, everything happened really quickly. Roger was calm and organised, finding dressings and comforting Phil's wife, who was shaking with fear and looked about to pass out herself. People appeared and took action. Phil needed expert surgery, and no-one was sure that it was available locally. His best option was to fly straight to the UK. Two men none of us had ever met before appeared in the living room with walkie talkies. They held up the next BA flight to London and we were put in a motorcade heading for the airport, the motorcade being a necessary safety measure when driving that road at night. I was in summer clothes with wet hair and sandals, but I had my medical bag and one of Roger's jumpers. Phil's condition remained fairly stable until we were about an hour from the UK, when his blood pressure dropped.

The pilot contacted Gatwick and when we landed, two surgeons came on board and took over Phil's care before anyone else was allowed off the plane. They explained that he did not have a lot of pain despite his wounds because neck injuries are able to swell without pressing on surrounding tissues. I called Lagos so that people knew we had both arrived in the UK alive and went to get some sleep before a visit to see Alex. I visited Phil in hospital in East Grinstead to check on him. The main danger was infection, but that had been avoided. When he finally went home, his main problem was damage that restricted movement of his jaw. I flew back to Lagos and JoKate.

Things did not improve. The next week, Roger went a funny colour during breakfast. I followed him upstairs where he was leaning against the bed clutching his chest. He turned an even funnier colour and said he had bad chest pain. I was about to ask if he would like some paracetamol when he fell on the bed still clutching his chest, which was apparently hurt a lot. I got my visiting bag, drew up some fortral and gave him an injection. He was now cold, clammy and unconscious. Yes, it was that fast. The only thing I knew to do for this situation was to give him intravenous morphine. I had done that once before for someone in heart failure and it worked instantly. I quickly ran through the options in my head: do nothing – looks as though he's about to die. Give him intravenous morphine and it doesn't work – wouldn't look good on my c.v. but after all that had happened I hardly cared. I gave him the intravenous morphine, very slowly. I shouted for Roger's houseboy and sent him to get help. He could see that there was a problem and sped off. Roger started to respond and was able to say that the pain had got a bit better. He wasn't so cold and clammy, but his blood pressure was very low, and his heart rate very, very slow.

I called my boss, to explain that I wouldn't be able to do morning surgery and asked him to come over with the portable ECG machine. From the ECG, we diagnosed a heart attack, later confirmed by a cardiologist who visited the house. When he was well enough, Roger called his employers in London. He had been advised not to fly to the

UK for six weeks but would work from home. It was a puzzle to us why someone so fit and healthy with no adverse family history, could have had a heart attack, age forty.

When we did get back to the UK, we found the answer. He had had acute pericarditis (an infection of the covering of the heart) which although not a heart attack, is just as dangerous. Meanwhile Alex's unhappiness at boarding school had become so severe, it was clear he had to leave, so while Roger flew back to work in Lagos, I spent time in Yorkshire arranging for Alex to live with friends and attend a local school until I could get back to the UK and find somewhere to live.

In Lagos, I gave notice on my job, at which I had not been a particularly regular attender this year due to the various emergencies. I spent time talking to David about JoKate. He was adamant that she would stay with him, his main arguments being that he had missed his three older children badly when his first marriage ended and that I was a terrible mother. He still felt extremely cross with me for leaving even though he was now in a committed relationship with a Ghanaian Princess who was living with him and taking good care of JoKate. I was in a weak position and knew how vindictive he could be but managed to wring out of him agreement that JoKate would come to stay with me in the UK when I had somewhere to live, at least for her holidays. And so, I returned to the UK to start again.

Chapter 6

A new direction

David and I separated in 1981 and he stayed in Nigeria with JoKate, having renewed his contract with ICL for another two years. I returned to live in South Yorkshire with Alex and started work as a locum GP in Sheffield. The house in Sheffield that David and I owned jointly was valued and David bought me out of my half share so that I could buy a property in Harthill, near to the comprehensive school Alex attended.

I found it hard to take General Practice seriously back in the UK, as I had such recent experience of Nigerians dying because of lack of sanitation and clean water, or because they relied on city witch doctors to treat a child for malaria. Although my first love was always General Practice, as a locum, I didn't know the patients and found it difficult to be sympathetic to their minor conditions.

Working in Nigeria had impressed me with the importance of things I had taken for granted: clean water, a sewage system, nutrition for young children, maternity care, safety at work, programmes to vaccinate against common infectious disease, health screening for common treatable conditions and effective hospital backup when being 'General' was no longer enough. Without these in place, western medicine was an expensive luxury. A colleague suggested that I took a higher degree in Public Health and with these newly opened eyes, I retrained in Public Health.

Fighting TB
I worked as a senior registrar in Public Health in Trent Regional Health Authority, attending lecture modules around the north of England and undertaking practical Public Health tasks in Worksop in North Nottinghamshire.

There were plans to build a new District General Hospital and I was tasked with reviewing the health needs of the local population, so that we would have approximately the right number of hospital beds per specialty. I don't think it had occurred to me that different towns needed different things from their hospitals, but of course, you need more orthopaedic services if you have a higher than average population of elderly people breaking their hips, or miners ruining their knees at work. It took a doctor to mediate when an ophthalmologist demanded a clinic with thirty yards of uninterrupted corridor space for eye testing, whereas standard hospital design assumed that you could manage with half that if you had a good mirror.

More immediate work showed up in the form of a case of open TB. We were notified by the local chest clinic of a patient who was a teacher at a local private boarding school and would have been infectious for the last half term before the summer holidays. It was Public Health's job to set up the programme of contact tracing. The school prepared a list of possible contacts, but the next stage was tricky. This was the end of the school year and half the children had gone abroad to join parents who were working overseas. I drafted a letter to be sent to all the parents, explaining that although the risk of infection was low, they should be alert to their child developing an unexplained cough or fever. Although vague, this was the best we could do since anyone who had been immunised against TB, would give a positive result for a skin test for TB infection. If anyone had contracted TB, the most likely form would be a chest infection, but pulmonary TB does not show up on a chest Xray during the first six weeks after infection. Tracking down each contact while the school was closed for the summer was not easy. Many of those we needed to reach were on holiday and not at their usual address. The secretarial staff were more than helpful and fortunately, no further TB infections were found.

Just as we were concluding this contact tracing programme, we were informed of a second case of open TB ('open' referred to the infection being spreadable through coughing) in a coal miner. He had been unwell for several months and had visited his GP several times, complaining of a cough. He had been given antibiotics. When he started coughing up blood stained sputum, he was finally taken seriously and sent to chest clinic. By this time, he was quite ill with pulmonary TB and was admitted to hospital. We set to contact tracing his colleagues at the mine, his social contacts and his family, at which point we discovered that he and his wife had a new baby. The baby was perfectly well, but not old enough to have been immunised against TB and so a possible carrier of infection (albeit this being a fairly remote risk). We were advised that we would need to contact trace everyone who has been in contact with the miner's wife (antenatal clinics, maternity ward, delivery suite) and their baby (health clinics, baby and toddler group), mainly because TB is an insidious disease that can begin with vague symptoms.

Our TB contact tracing programme now covered almost eight percent of the population and was causing alarm. We did what we could to allay fear and questioned the professional advice that led to such a huge programme based on a relatively small risk. I was, perhaps, more wary of TB infection than some, due to my experience of expat infections in Lagos, and before that, the death of a nine-year-old child from miliary (blood borne) TB on my ward when I was a junior doctor.

When we thought we had turned a corner and covered all the TB contact tracing a small town would ever need, we were notified of a third case of open TB. This time, the notification came from Rampton Hospital, where an eighty-two-year-old patient had died. All patient deaths in a secure hospital are subject to a post-mortem and this had revealed pulmonary TB. By now, the chest physician, chest clinic nurses and I were wondering what had hit us. Contact tracing would not be easy. The staff at Rampton (prison officers) don't agree to anything without consulting their union (the POA) and the POA said no. Nevertheless, we hired a mobile Xray unit and placed it on site at their disposal. It was up to them whether they used it. Very few did. Relatively few patients within Rampton had been in contact with the deceased, but they could not be brought to a clinic in large numbers, so I went in with my stethoscope. I had never seen so many keys on one person as on the officers who escorted me around. The keys themselves seemed to be used to display superior power. I did not like the atmosphere in there.

By the time we had offered screening for TB to nine percent of the population of our district, we considered our job done. For all that effort, no further cases of TB were found, and worry was caused to a lot of people.

My Public Health mentor at region asked me to investigate the epidemiology of chlamydia. A new consultant in GU Medicine in another town, had begun testing every female patient for this infection and treating them with antibiotics. This was not usual practice in the UK in 1984, although things were a little more proactive in the

USA. His local laboratory queried the amount of work they were being asked to undertake, and the consultant himself was asking for more resources to enable him to screen even more women at risk of this infection. My job was to undertake independent research into the costs and benefits of screening for chlamydia and to make recommendations. Research of this sort before we had the internet, meant hours in the main library retrieving articles in GU medicine journals in the UK and the USA. My conclusion was that there was a case for detecting and treating chlamydial infections that would be costly but worthwhile. In the course of my research, I was reading about a new set of symptoms presenting at genitourinary clinics in the USA, that had no name (although it would soon be called HTLV1) and no treatment but seemed to be killing people. I mentioned in my report that perhaps we should be preparing for this as well as worrying about the laboratory costs of detecting chlamydia. How prescient was I?

Search for my real mother continues

In Worksop, I was also a volunteer helping to set up a refuge for women escaping domestic violence. Most of the other volunteers were social workers. During a fundraising event, I mentioned my failure to find my birth mother. By the following Monday, I was a case again, with an allocated social worker. Maureen chatted me through my progress so far and the positive and negative results that a search can have. Realising that I was, in fact, prepared for most eventualities, she started enquiries with the local authority that had dealt with my adoption. I was SO excited. But of course, there were no records. It was suggested that they been lost in a fire at Willesden Council offices years before.

I grieved for the lost opportunity and wondered whether fate was telling me not to search. There always seemed to be a brick wall. Stuck at the bottom of a roller coaster of emotions, I sort of gave up.

Then in 1987, I read *Lost Children* by Polly Toynbee. Her book described how the children and mothers affected by forced adoptions felt – bereft, yearning and somehow unfinished being the most persistent and disabling emotions that follow us through all the situations of our lives. I became very angry when some of the adoptive parents described in the book blocked their children's attempts to find their original families. Her research revealed that most of the mothers who had given up children for adoption, did want to find them. Polly postulated that adopted children have a right to know their origins. This was a revelation to me. Reflecting on what I had read and the experiences of other adopted children, I adjusted from feeling guilty that I wanted to know, to being angry that I didn't. I climbed back onto the rollercoaster.

Maureen, my social worker, had managed to obtain a copy of my original birth certificate on which my mother was recorded as a shorthand typist and gave her address as Salisbury. My name was Rosemary Jean and my birth was registered in Tunbridge Wells. Apparently, I did not have a father. Well, his identity was left blank on the certificate. In the margin, the registrar had written 'adopted.' It was quite an overwhelming feeling having the proof that I did have a real mother and it somehow made me feel authentic for the first time. She had been twenty-three when I was born and gave her address as a house in Salisbury. I went to see it. It was a fairly large brick-built house. My heart was pounding. Heaven knows what the occupants would think about me sitting outside for so long just looking. So, I knocked on the door. Explaining why I was there, the woman who came to the door looked perplexed and then sympathetic. She invited me into the kitchen. She and her husband had just moved in. I told her the whole story, and when she heard my birth mother's surname she went 'oh' and covered her mouth with her hand. 'Wait,' she said and left the room. My heart was pounding alarmingly loudly now. What she brought back into the room were the deeds to the house. There was my mother's surname. From the dates on the deeds, we worked out that her father (my grandfather) had bought the house in the 1950s and had lived there until the year before, when he died, and it was sold. Since my mother had given this as her address in 1945, we assumed that the family had been renting the house before they bought it. I could not hide my excitement at getting new information, but the new owners of the house did not have any information about other, living family members. Everything had been handled by solicitors. Still, I felt as though I was a step closer.

Between 1975 and 2002, the only opportunity for mothers and their adopted children to find each other, although legal, was through private detective work or voluntary agencies that created their own registers to help the hundreds of mothers and children who had been separated. With the bit between my teeth now, I joined NORCAP, one of the national registers. When both mother and child register, they could put us in touch with each other. They had all the appropriate policies and procedures to minimise problem reactions when people were reunited because there can be difficulties as well as bonuses when a match is found. I also joined a NORCAP support group in

London for adopted people engaged in a search. We all clung to the belief that the truth is more acceptable than fantasy, because we all needed to know about our roots. But of course, for me NORCAP could not find a match.

Since we were still in the pre-digital age, all my searching was done laboriously, by post. Clutching at straws, I chased up information about my Christening. Dad had written down for me the name of the church where I was Christened, the date and the name of the minister. Hoping that the church had done a better job of keeping their records safe since 1946, I waited for a letter in the post. It arrived. They could not find any record of my Christening in that year. They were very sorry. I oscillated between fury, sadness and perplexity. Why were all these trails leading nowhere?

I took a tip from one of the women at the NORCAP support group. She had traced a marriage certificate for her birth mother, so found her new surname and then the birth certificates for children born after she was married. This gave her a recent address and NORCAP trained social worker had agreed to make the first tentative approach to her birth mother. I set about doing the same and was stunned to find my own birth mother's marriage certificate and the birth certificate for two children of the marriage. At this point, fate gave up its persistent attempts to thwart my search. The social worker from NORCAP wrote to me in April 1987, asking me to call her, as she had had an enquiry from my mother. MY MOTHER. I shook, I could hardly take the information in. I drank three large brandies. They had no effect. This was such tremendous news that I could not sleep or think or anything.

The NORCAP social worker, also called Linda, sent me a copy of the letter my mother had written when she registered with NORCAP – with my mother's agreement of course. She said that she was shocked to learn that I was searching for her and would have been happy just to know that I was alive, well and happy. This more or less reflected my motives in searching too. She went on 'the prospect of coming face to face with her presented me with a problem. I promised her parents I would never ever encroach upon their private world, and I would still stand by that undertaking, in spite of my own very deep yearning to show her that I never stopped loving her or missing her from my life. They were kind enough to give her a new home and a good life – which at that time I could see no sign of happening if she remained with me – and I still feel that if we two were to make contact again, it must be with her parents' full consent and approval.' And she still thought that I was called Rosemary, as she had Christened me.

I was having none of it. I was 42 with two children of my own and not about to involve my adoptive parents in this reunion. In fact, I didn't involve anyone else. I insisted that we meet up, at which point I discovered that my mother (Doris) did not drive because her husband, who had died recently, did not want her to learn. I had views on that. We did meet. From what Doris said, it sounded as though she had accepted that no-one would marry her if she kept me. When she met her future husband, she told him about my birth but promised never to mention it again. She kept a small black and white photo of me and cried each year when it was the anniversary of my birth. She and her husband were publicans and had three children, my half brothers and sister. She felt that he had been very good to marry her and that she had not tried to find me while he was alive, because it would have been disloyal. I said nothing.

I met my half-sister and brothers and got on well with two of them. I met their partners and their many children, my mother's siblings, their partners and all their children. They were a hugely welcoming family, considering that they had not even known that I existed. Doris had been the eldest sister in a family of four children. She was quite a lot older than her two sisters, who were aware that there had been a row, that Doris had gone away, and that their father had forbidden them ever to mention her again. They didn't know why. Doris also had a brother – his father's pride and joy. But the brother had been damaged during an anaesthetic given when he was having his tonsils out when he was eight. He was left with a considerable mental disability. His father never got over it.

Time with Doris was spent catching up and showing each other photos of our lives, except she did not seem particularly interested in my life or my children. I started to realise that she still saw me as the curly headed cherub, aged fifteen months and could not adjust to the strong independent woman I had become. Over and over, she would ask how I could forgive her for giving me up to adoption. Over and over, I explained that I knew things were different then, and that she had little option. In the end, I understood that it was not my forgiveness that was the issue. That she could not forgive herself.

I had my fiftieth birthday in September 1995. I decided to take a stand. Doris and I were meeting regularly and while not close, were getting on. It was time to tell my children that they had another grandmother. They were fascinated by the story of how we met and were happy to meet Doris. I invited them all to my birthday party, along with friends from work, and my sister, half-brothers and adoptive brother. It was an extraordinary party. I had not, though, told my adoptive parents about finding Doris. In my mind, this was the kindest option. In fact, I suspect it was cowardice. When I heard myself telling Alex and JoKate not to mention Doris to their other Nanna, I knew it was wrong. Betty and Bernard had to be told.

Roger and I had a trip to visit my parents planned, to coincide with me attending a friend's wedding. Being a kind, brave soul, Roger agreed to tell Betty and Bernard about Doris while I was away at the wedding. He described this task as 'herding cats', never being able to get them both in the same room at the same time and unable to get a word in edgeways. But he did tell them. Betty shed a few tears. Bernard said not much. When I got back from the wedding, I was told by Betty that they knew I had found Doris, they understood why I needed to do so, but please could we never speak of it again. End of story.

Doris's home was over three hour's drive from where I lived. She had weak ankles (so do I) and would not go out at night in case she fell. I had a busy day job and worked several evenings as a board member on London charities. I had two teenage children. My adoptive parents lived a long way away and were becoming elderly, needing visits every month or two. It was difficult fitting it all in. Eventually, I persuaded Doris to take the train and visit us at our house in south London. On the day she was due to arrive, the crunch came. I called in the morning to check that she was ready to catch the train. It was 11am. She was very drunk.

All she could say was 'how could you forgive me? How could you forgive me?' over and over. 'Doris,' I said 'this is not good for you. Let's have a break from meeting up and let things settle.'

Next, a search for my birth father

Over the years since I had found Doris, I had cautiously asked about the identity of my father. For a long time, she was evasive. Then one day she told me that he had been an airman from a family that had a market garden business in Kent, but he had died in action while she was pregnant. I followed this news up but could not find any evidence that he existed. I double checked with her that I had got his name right. She admitted that she had made the story up. She furnished me with another tale about who my father was, that also turned out to be fictitious. I found the lies hard to bear but assumed that she possibly did not know who my father was but could not face that fact. I stopped asking.

Sometime later, Doris volunteered the information I had waited for. She said that while she was working in an administrative job in the army, she had had a serious relationship with a soldier. In 1944, he had ended it and she was very unhappy. Doris spent Christmas and New Year with her uncle and his wife – her father's older brother. She was not getting on with her parents and somehow circumstances led to an affair with her uncle and a pregnancy. For this, she got all the blame and was not allowed back to her parents' house. Her sisters were not told why and were not allowed to mention her name in the house thereafter.

In view of the sensitivity of this information about my natural father, I employed a researcher recommended by NORCAP to look for information on him. She found his death certificate easily; he had died in 1987 at his daughter's house. His wife was also dead, and her address had also been given as that of their daughter who still lived at the same address. Through tracing Doris and telling my adoptive family and friends about her, I felt that I had emerged from the shadows. It would be good to know more about my father, but there was a chance that his daughter did not know of my existence. This may have been an old family wound that had healed. I felt it best to end my search there, leaving just the one stone unturned. Incest is a risky thing for the children, resulting in unacceptably high levels of genetic abnormality, often manifest as low intelligence. I think I escaped that one.

It was not until 2002 that the government created a central register enabling adoptees and their natural families to contact each other under controlled circumstances.

A new opportunity

While I waited for a desirable consultant post to be advertised, there was another NHS reorganisation. All consultant posts were frozen. There was no certainty that they would be unfrozen for months, if not years and I became impatient. With my, 'I am a doctor, how hard can it be?' arrogance, I applied for a newly created post of Unit General Manager in Riverside Health Authority in London. I was slightly alarmed when I was successful and found myself with a hefty annual budget and hundreds of staff to manage. I was taught to read budget sheets and how to speak in public and on TV, both of which were vital managerial skills. I had to learn how to speed read or delegate the mountains of paper that passed through my office.

I began with fine principles of keeping patient welfare and accessibility as my main aims for the services for which I was responsible. Our management team managed community health services for Kensington, Chelsea and Westminster, community dental and chiropody services, hospital and community services for elderly people and services for people with learning disabilities. We were constantly pulled into tortuous disputes over staff grades, disciplinary procedures and contracting out support services. It was hard to keep patient welfare at the forefront of decision making.

Huge amounts of time had to be invested to liaise with Social Service Departments in three London Boroughs, as we jointly implemented a programme to close long stay hospitals in the Epsom cluster and rehouse people with learning disabilities into their borough of origin, including those in central London. There were mounting community concerns about our District Health Authority's plans to rebuild St. Stephens (now the Westminster and Chelsea Hospital) and I was involved in arrangements for decanting services from Westminster Hospital while the rebuild took place. Simultaneously, I took the lead on developing one of the first software programmes for community nursing. Most days entailed six meetings, for which I had to prepare, and afterwards, I had to action the things we had agreed. I had to take files home to read and had reports and papers to write in the evenings and on weekends. Management turned out not to be the easy job I had thought, and I yearned for the simplicity of General Practice.

Lives get busier

Roger's job was equally hectic, because doing business as an insurance broker involved (apparently) entertaining clients regularly. The entertaining involved eating, drinking and attending sports events for which his company paid. I would have been disciplined and sacked for that in the NHS. Roger was also in great demand as skipper for Lloyds Yacht *Lutine*. He would be booked to take clients sailing for weekends in the Solent, for which he had to victual the boat in advance and although there was a paid skipper, much of the passage planning and preparation fell to Roger.

David and I had both been divorced before and knew that the experience could be both bad and expensive, so resolved to work on agreeing the terms and sorting it out ourselves without a solicitor. Roger had stayed in Nigeria until he was offered a job at head office in London. Since his marriage was over, he decided that he would also agree a divorce settlement with his wife and not involve solicitors.

By 1988, Alex had left school and moved to London to live with his father, Aristophanes. David returned to a UK based job with Florence, to whom he was now married. They bought a house in Woking. JoKate went to Frensham Heights School. Roger and I now lived together in London and I had secured a qualification in Public Health. All our parents were now elderly and having health problems, requiring regular weekend visits to them in Devon. With two ex-spouses to liaise with and three teenage children, we were kept busy. I tried to stop smoking several times in 1988 but there wasn't really any space for that.

We bought a time share in a canal boat that gave us three weeks' peace each year. Cruising at four miles an hour through tranquil countryside was the complete antidote to our lives in London. We took our two cats with us and whichever children said they were free. Friends met us and stayed for a few nights. We slept. A lot. Only interrupted by the cats who had the run of the boat, slept on our bed or spent the nights hunting on the canal tow path. Our canal holiday in March gave us a rare opportunity to talk things through. Our divorces were both finalised. We decided to get married in July, in a small ceremony with just our three children as witnesses. Then, for our honeymoon the five of us would go away together to a self-catering villa in Spain. I booked Villa Linda Vista.

Tragic news
Then, on 23rd July 1988, David had a heart attack and died. He was fifty-three. He and Florence had been on holiday in Scotland with friends. Florence called me that evening, so shocked that she was barely able to speak. She knew that JoKate was at our home for the weekend and wanted me to tell her that her father had died. I could not absorb the information and kept asking her how? Why? As I put the phone down, Roger came out of the kitchen and when he saw me asked, 'What has happened?' I did not want to say the words. My mind was telling me that I could have imagined it, and that saying that David was dead would make it true. In a daze, I told him, but before we could think what to do next, JoKate was on the stairs asking what we were talking about. I sat down with her. There was no easy way to explain or wrap this up. And I had no answers.

Friends who were with Florence in Scotland, called later to say that they would bring her home to Woking the next day and asked if we would be there to meet them.

When they arrived from the airport, we had to help Florence into the house. Her friends looked traumatised and left quickly. As word spread, people began to phone. No sooner had we hung up on one shocked friend or relative, than another called. It was so hard. We had to tell David's first wife, Sylvia, his mother, Kate, and his three children from his marriage to Sylvia. All we knew was that he was out walking in the Scottish hills with friends and fell down with a heart attack. It was that quick.

David had told Florence to call myself and Roger if ever anything happened to him. He knew that she could trust us. Her house now filled with friends, our children, Florence's family, David's family, neighbours and David's colleagues from work. In between taking care of the children and making huge pots of bolognaise sauce to feed everyone, we talked to Florence about arranging David's funeral and shared out jobs to everyone. Sylvia Benson (David's first wife) and I began to choose hymns and organise the service. David had been a Catholic when he was married to Sylvia, so she tried a couple of priests he had known. One turned out to have died some time before and the second would have come for the service, but had a marriage already booked. So, we decided that the Catholic fates were not in our favour.

Through London Lighthouse I had gained considerable experience of organising personal but non-religious funerals and eventually, we found a delightful Humanist celebrant for the funeral service. He was really helpful and brought his wife with him to meet us in advance so that he could find out what David had been like. The celebrant had a strong Sheffield accent, which we thought was appropriate, because David had lived in

Sheffield for nearly twenty years. The only difficulty was that the celebrant was completely deaf. He explained that this wouldn't matter because during the service he only needed to be able to communicate with the person playing the funeral music.

Florence, who is a Ghanaian princess, was soon supported by a large number of fellow countrymen and women most of whom who we did not know. They began their traditional grieving procedure – a sort of wailing – by ululating. Whilst accepting the importance of her cultural customs, the children found this particular one very upsetting and we decided, on balance, that we had to say something. There was no more ululating.

David had died on a Saturday. There was a Scottish post-mortem on Monday and his body was flown back on Tuesday. Roger and I were getting married on Thursday, the cremation was booked for Friday, the day we were due to go on honeymoon with the children. Roger and I simply had to take a break on Wednesday to go into work to sort out our offices as we would be away the following two weeks. My colleagues at work were sympathetic but told me later that I was not making much sense that day. We also slipped in a hurried visit to a second-hand shop in Lordship Lane to buy a wedding ring.

Charlie, David's best friend from Sheffield, arrived to help with the arrangements. Florence found her favourite photo of David for the order of service and selected his favourite music from the tapes in his car. Charlie and I took them to the funeral directors to finalise the order of service. David would be buried in his favourite T shirt: pale blue with an intricate design. If you looked closely you could see that the design was a series of line drawings of people having group sex (David called it a gang bang). The funeral director asked if we would like to see the body, which was lying in their chapel of rest. I hesitated but knew that it would be best for me to do so as I was still shocked and struggling to keep it rational. David's body was cold. So cold. But my overriding feeling on seeing him was fear. Fear that he would wake up and attack me for believing that he was dead when he wasn't and that I had done nothing about it. Charlie put an arm round me, and we went back to the funeral director's office.

Hymns chosen, coffin chosen, order of service explained, the funeral director asked us for the tapes for the music that would be played at the beginning and end of the service. 'Oh, just one point,' he added 'the chap who does the music is blind, but it doesn't matter. The person taking the service can...' I briefly had a vision of potential disaster with the deaf man, the blind man and eight grief-stricken teenagers, let alone the rest of us. I opened my mouth then closed it again. Life is bizarre sometimes and best left to sort itself out.

A sudden and unexpected death often evokes a feeling of disbelief. After much discussion and wine, we decided that we would bring David's body back to his home on the morning of the funeral so that anyone who wanted could have a moment to say goodbye. We bought red roses for Florence and each of the children to place inside the coffin with him. More people arrived. 'What will he do without his dictionary?' asked Florence in a panic. We placed his biggest and favourite, The Shorter Oxford Dictionary that he called the SOD, in the coffin with him.

The four Mrs. Bensons always got on together well, which I always thought rather annoyed David, who would have preferred that we fell out a lot and fought over him. I think he was slightly worried that we were comparing notes. We often were. David's mum, Kate Benson, took responsibility for getting the eight children we had from various marriages to the funeral.

There must have been a hundred of us at the service, for which we were allowed about twenty minutes by the crematorium. The Humanist celebrant read out words written by Florence and the children and there were no hitches. Everyone drove back to the house, where we had a proper wake, and all said how we remembered David and what he meant to us. Exhausted, Roger and I drove our three children back to our house in Dulwich to prepare for our wedding the next day.

The four Mrs Bensons

Being sensible, David had written a will. Less sensibly, he had appointed his bank manager as Executor. Florence was agitated when we returned from our honeymoon. The bank manager had called around to talk about the will and had persuaded her to sell the house. Moreover, she had signed a document authorising him to sell on her behalf, leaving her with no say over the sale price. We smelt a rat. Florence did not want to sell the house. She could not really say how he had persuaded her to do so and was now very worried about where she would live. In fact, she hadn't been in any state to think it through and was alarmed when the bank manager wrote to say he could get a quick sale at a price that was way below market value. Florence couldn't face seeing him on her own, so we all went: the four Mrs Bensons. Sylvia Benson, David's first wife, me, Linda

Benson, his second wife, Florence Benson, his widow and Kate Benson his mum.

We sat outside the bank manager's office in Woking. When we were shown in his face dropped. 'Mrs. Benson?' he murmured in a rather lost way. 'Yes,' we all said. He sat for a moment with his mouth open, unable to speak. So, I launched in, explaining that Florence did not want to sell her house and would not be making any big decisions for at least a month. If she did decide to sell the house in the future, she would not be using the bank's services. He began to reason with us in a condescending manner, but we were furious with him. We had talked this through and believed that he was an arrogant and incompetent man and possibly unscrupulous. He wilted under the tirade of three Mrs Bensons (Florence was too polite to disagree with a bank manager in those days). When we stormed out, we felt light as air and very proud of ourselves. Florence was amazed that we'd managed to sort it out 'without a man.' Oh dear.

Roger is good with money, so Florence asked him to check through the bank manager's application for probate. David had left the house to her in its entirety, and through his death, the outstanding amount on the mortgage would be covered by life insurance. As his spouse, she was entitled to inherit the house free from death duty, but the bloody bank manager appeared not to know this and had included the value of the house as a taxable asset. As a result of this mistake, he told Florence that she owed an enormous amount in death duty. She did not have the money.

We called the bank manager. He was very rude, as he never made mistakes and now regarded us as troublemakers. We called the relevant tax office and explained the situation. They said that they could not deal with us. They could only talk to the Executor of the will. We called the bank's head office and eventually spoke to someone who, while not accepting that any fault of any kind could be attributed to the bank in any way, did transfer the responsibility for the execution of the will to someone at Head Office, who put things right. Still furious, I asked for a copy of the bank's quality standards for probate and execution of wills. They had none. The only national body with oversight of banking practice excludes Executorship from their remit. I contacted *Which?* magazine and they included our story in their monthly publication, but this did not change anything. Years later, still enraged by their bad practice; we named a particularly unpleasant part of the garden 'Midland Bank.' Only then did we get a result: they changed their name to HSBC.

I wrote a poem after David died,

GONE
The last battle
was my refusal to fight.
That really got to you.
worse than disagreement,
worse than stubborn silence.
No way you could engage me,
at last.

I wanted to reach
beyond the highs and lows.
To find the thrills of peace.
But I knew that to you
the fights were proof of life.

It isn't good without you here
for me to refuse to fight with.

An important new Lighthouse

After four years, my belief that working as an NHS manager was easier than working as a doctor, was in tatters. The opportunity arose to apply for the post of Director of Public Health in the same Health Authority and I applied. There has always been a pressing need for Public Health input to service planning in central London and now we needed to assess how to respond to the demand for services for people with HIV.

Discrimination against gay people had not yet been made illegal and when the first cases of HIV infection and AIDS were diagnosed in the UK, the existing hostility became dangerous in many parts of the country. Gay men moved to places that felt safer. For many, this was London. We experienced a sudden and sustained increase in demand for services, but it was patchy, and difficult to extrapolate how this would pan out in the future. An effective bush telegraph meant that people with symptoms of the HIV disease knew where they would be treated with dignity and sympathy. The GU medicine clinics at St. Stephens' Hospital on Fulham Road and St. Mary's Hospital, Paddington were constantly packed out. In the early days, there were also two consultants in these hospitals whose adherence to the Hippocratic Oath still guided them: Dr Tony Pinching, a consultant in Immunology at St. Mary's and Dr Brian Gazzard, consultant in General Medicine and gastroenterology at St. Stephens'.

In the early days of the epidemic, we did not have a blood test to identify the HIV virus and did not know what the pattern of disease would be or what the life expectancy was for people infected. We had to more or less guess what services would be needed. We were in the early days of computing and many laboratories and clinics recorded cases of HIV related disease, but we did not know how many of the recordings were duplicates without manually cross-checking names for each clinic and laboratory. Suddenly, the confidentiality of such data became really important and we quickly devised new training for data handling and protection.

The Chief Medical Officer, Sir Donald Acheson, set up a national AIDS committee as did every Regional and District Health Authority and most Local Authorities. These consumed enormous amounts of time but served the extremely useful functions of informing managers of HIV facts as they emerged, of improving their attitude to people with HIV and standardising the terminology that was acceptable. In the early days, phrases such as 'gay plague' and 'AIDS sufferers' went uncorrected. Once we explained why these were inappropriate, senior managers all started to use more appropriate terms ('people with HIV') and this filtered through to everyone else. Negative attitudes to people with HIV were as dangerous as the disease itself, in many ways. We had such tricky issues to discuss; prevention of infection through the supply of free condoms, including in prisons; the provision of clean needles for injecting drug users and safe disposal of used needles and sourcing safe Factor 8 for haemophiliacs. Meetings could get heated.

Prevention of cross infection, always important in hospitals, became of life and death importance. Whereas a quick wipe of equipment with an antiseptic had sufficed in most departments, the resilience of this virus meant that every procedure and piece of equipment had to be reviewed and new procedures put in place.

Some consultants were so alarmed by the resilience of the HIV virus that they feared treating infected patients. I was one of the people who would be sent in to have a quiet word and explain that their contract required them to treat everyone. These conversations often revealed strong prejudice against people who were gay. I could not understand the source of this, and no-one seemed to be able to explain it to me.

People with HIV or belonging to a group at increased risk of infection, were facing extensive discrimination in housing, employment and insurance. When we were aware of this, we first tried to expose the problem and get those responsible to articulate the reasons. Illogical prejudice does not always withstand public exposure. Many leaders in the gay community had extremely good connections in politics, business and the entertainment industry and let's just say that we made good of this.

Many agencies looked to the NHS for information on HIV and for training for their staff. We had HIV training programmes for NHS staff operating at full stretch for months and realised that we needed to extend training to many of the people working in Social Services and Housing Departments. It sometimes felt as though HIV had infected everything we did. Just when you thought you had covered every eventuality, there would be a desperate phone call: Afro-Caribbean District Nurses had participated fully in training, but their husbands would not allow them to treat patients with HIV and we had missed the staff of the mobile library who were now refusing to accept books returned by people with HIV. Dentists asked for help with improving their infection control procedures and we had to approach tattoo parlours and ask them to do the same. We were made aware of funeral directors who had refused to provide a service for people who had died of AIDS, or if they did, made inappropriate and ostentatious displays of sealed body bags and invented unscientific rules about who could handle the coffin and how. By June 1987, the number of people known to be infected was doubling every month. As numbers rose, all blood spills had to be treated as potentially infected, meaning training and revision of procedures for sporting activities. And on it went.

As the epidemic progressed, people were dying from AIDS related disease. The NHS had always been better at saving lives than caring for the dying, whereas the hospice movement and community terminal care teams had huge expertise. Dame Cicely Saunders had led the way in the movement but decided that people with HIV disease would not be offered hospice care. No amount of reasoning would change her mind and as she still had a strong influence on hospice policy and major funding sources, we reached an impasse.

And so, in North Kensington, a group of determined people decided to set up a centre for meeting the challenge of AIDS. It would be called London Lighthouse and perhaps because I chaired the AIDS committee for the District Health Authority, I was invited to join the Council. Lighthouse would be a centre for meeting the challenge of AIDS with a mortuary, palliative care ward, community services, 'one stop' advice services covering housing, insurance and financial support for people affected by HIV and AIDS.

Many public figures were courageous in openly supporting us when this was a risky publicity statement. When we opened, we provided much needed services in an inspiring environment that felt safe to service users, but we also provided a focus for the media, largely because our Director, Christopher Spence, had personal experience of friends dying from the disease and was determined, articulate, unflappable and very human.

Lighthouse Council meetings were scary, because often we didn't know whether we would have funding for more than the next three months. The debate was lively, given that the mix of Council members included the chair of the National Aids Trust, a member of the House of Lords, the national Director of the Prison Service (with armed protection officers), service users and members of staff. As Council members we were involved with Lighthouse service users in many ways between meetings. One of Lighthouse's strengths was the superb quality of funerals – of which there were many – the style of which borrowed from the best traditions of many cultures. One of the saddest facts about the community response to HIV and AIDS was the way that many leaders of organised religion rejected people at the point at which they needed spiritual support most. Lighthouse was having none of it. The community of staff and service users talked frankly about death and dying. The planning stage of many of the funerals was actually fun. I stopped feeling apprehensive about going to funerals because they were stylish and there was peace.

Chapter 7

The twelve steps

I have a huge number of friends and an enormous family; Roger and our children and grandchildren, my adoptive parents, my brother and wider family, my birth mother and half siblings and their families, two ex-husbands, their ex and new wives and associated children, Roger and his family and his daughter from his first marriage. They are all people that I love and need. Maybe having been given away once, I have insured against being abandoned again?

But every single relationship brings worries and dilemmas at some time. Life is a series of risks taken and lessons learned and in 1988, I sometimes felt as though I had dived into a tempestuous sea. At other times, I felt nothing. Work could be all consuming, there was a lot of family stuff and our new marriage to take care of. David's sudden death had a serious impact on the mental stability of the children. He had been a very strong personality and at times, a bully. We all loved and feared him in different ways. I was on the management group or board of several charitable organisations, all dealing with emotionally loaded issues.

In autumn 1988, I faced the fact that I was struggling as a parent, wife and colleague because of my drinking. Being a logical person, I just tried to stop. It didn't work. I tried to stop smoking. It lasted until I started drinking again. I was not accustomed to this sort of failure and the idea of getting help crossed my mind. As a doctor with a mental health problem, I decided to go to the top and consult a professor. He took details of my drinking habit and tested my blood for liver damage. There was no damage. He suggested controlled drinking. I had tried that and failed many times. He did not suggest controlled smoking.

I lurched on, developing a pattern of drinking fairly normal amounts of wine some nights, then about four nights a week, I would wait until Roger was in bed and drink whisky while I wrote reports or read documents for work until I was falling asleep. If I had drunk so much of his whisky that the level in the bottle would be noticeable, I was flexible enough to move on to brandy or Pernod, although Pernod was not a smart choice because it goes cloudy when you water it down. If my hangover was really bad, I would have the next night without alcohol. Thus, I somehow forced myself to cope through 1989 and into 1990.

That summer, in 1990, our offices were moved from Westminster to Parsons Green. We were next door to a pub. I had a 5pm meeting with Brian, to discuss ongoing funding for research into mental health and HIV disease. It was a very hot day and he suggested that we go for a drink next door rather than sit in the office. I said okay, but not alcohol, as I was still suffering from the night before. His eyebrows shot up.

We drank lime and soda and sorted out the funding issue. Brian gently probed whether suffering a hangover for more than eighteen hours was an exception. I had to say no, it wasn't. And then he offered to help. I explained that I had already tried help and that controlled drinking didn't work for me. But Brian was not talking about that. He was talking about sobriety. He was talking about abstinence.

Within twenty-four hours, Brian had arranged for a specialist addiction counsellor to call me to arrange an appointment. I saw her the next day and went through the history of my drinking. She explained that alcohol is the most efficient anaesthetic for emotional pain and that alcohol addiction is an illness that tells you that you have not got it, both of which made sense to me. She asked why I wanted to give up now and I explained that I could see myself descending to a level at which I would not be a proper mother or grandmother. 'Hmm,' she said. If you are serious about giving up, you are more likely to succeed if the reason you do it is for yourself.

I left with homework: to list the good and bad things about drinking and not drinking. At our next meeting, we talked about those lists. I expected the hardest things about giving up would be stopping my habit of secret drinking in the late evening and refusing alcohol in company. I can help with that, she said, if you really think you can put as much effort into stopping as you put in now, to hide your drinking and coping with the hangovers. I could. I was ready for this. Excited almost. She did warn me that it might not be plain sailing. People change when they stop drinking the amount I had been consuming. Relationships that have developed during your drinking days, do not always survive sobriety. Living with a sober partner who does not have secrets or hangovers, can upset the balance. She invited me to set a date to stop drinking. Tomorrow I asked? No, she said. Because in a month it will be Christmas and it might be wise to have a bit of sobriety under your belt before you try a Christmas sober. Do not set yourself up to fail. Fix a date after Christmas.

And so, I did. Thirteenth of January 1991. As a general rule, success at stopping harmful drinking is more likely to follow if you spend as much time sorting yourself out as you used to do drinking. My counsellor, a wise person who had coached a lot of people through stopping, suggested that I might pop into an AA meeting. 'I go myself sometimes. They have a really positive atmosphere. I find the recovering alcoholics there very intelligent. You probably won't like it, but it is worth considering.' Which was exactly the right approach to get me to give it a try. Brian stepped in again, 'You might like someone to go with you for the first meeting,' he said and introduced me to Emma.

I stopped drinking as planned on 13th January. The first evening was okay, because I had had occasional evenings without a drink before. Roger was encouraging but perplexed. He had not seen me drunk very often and was unaware of the level of the problem. I explained it all in stages, and I needed his help. All the alcohol in the house was put in one place in a cupboard in the dining room so that I wasn't opening a cupboard and seeing a bottle I had not expected. For a week, I came home from work and just sat on the sofa while he cooked supper. Then I went to bed. We turned down invitations if I didn't think I would be comfortable around people drinking alcohol. It had been my habit to buy booze in the supermarket when doing the family shop. I stopped doing that and Roger bought his own supply. He is one of those people who can have a cigarette at a party and then forget that he's got them for three months. He would drink a glass of wine with supper and then put the bottle away. Both quite beyond my understanding.

Emma took me to my first AA meeting. I had worried so much about being seen going into the meeting, but after sauntering between two concrete buildings, round a dark corner and up some poorly lit stairs I realised that it was actually quite hard to find an AA meeting unless you were looking carefully and knew the address. There are no signs. The meeting was packed and friendly. Anyone for whom it was their first meeting was invited to put up their hand. We were given applause and told that this had been the hardest part. It gets easier. There was a reading from the AA big book and then someone shared the story of their drinking, when they stopped and how things had changed for them. I was shocked by how many of the things they did, I did too: hiding bottles, telling lies about being ill when I had a hangover, making sure I was half way drunk before going to a party, taking bottles into hotel rooms when away from home, buying a double of spirits at the bar for myself when getting a round in.

Abstinence, thoughts and feelings

My other worry was being recognised, as we were on my work territory. But anonymity means just that. Only first names are used. I did not recognise anyone, and no-one recognised me. The rest of the AA meeting consisted of people taking turns to share their thoughts on sobriety with the main speaker. I was shocked again by feeling that I had something in common with every one of them, so much so that it felt like coming home.

Afterwards I went to a coffee bar with Emma and some of her friends. I asked how often they went to meetings. The general response was twice a week once you were feeling fairly confident about stopping, but in the first few months, go for as many evenings as you used to drink. That felt like a tall order but driving home, I realised that I had actually enjoyed the meeting more than some of the charity work I usually did after work. I found the booklet of AA meetings in London and checked them against my crowded diary.

I saw the addiction counsellor one more time after my AA meeting. She asked how I felt about it, and I described that at some length after which she said, 'I didn't ask what you thought. I asked how you felt.' Thoughts and feelings. I was forty-five and I did not know the difference.

I started attending different meetings around central London, including one for women only. It is important for your recovery to speak at least once at a meeting – to be taking part rather than sitting as an observer. It's about being committed. There are few limits on what you say when you share, although it is recommended that you don't speak unless you have been sober for twenty-four hours and you are not supposed to swear.

Emma became my sponsor and took me through the twelve steps. This requires honesty about not just your drinking but anything significant about your behaviour in the past that is still bugging you, then teaches you to let it go. If you cannot let things go, resentment can build up. Resentment is a strong risk factor for drinking too much. I carry the AA Serenity Prayer with me still, twenty-eight years later. I simply have the sort of personality that tends to pick up resentments and the prayer helps me to let go of them.

It's a spiritual illness and the God word puts some people off AA but is there for a reason. Many drinking alcoholics tend to think that they are always right, in charge and in control, a bit like a god. This is not healthy or respectful. Part of the way that AA works is to get us to accept that we are not those things. That there is a higher power ('God' for short) who is in charge. It isn't us. It doesn't have to be a traditional religion, just a power greater than ourselves.

Looking back sober at the pattern of my drinking, it became clear that much of it was a response to emotionally fraught life events. There had been years when I had had a serious change to deal with every month: a birth, a death, moving house, marriages, divorces, changing jobs. As these events piled on top of each other, my mental health wobbled. The first year of sobriety is hard, like the first year after bereavement. Most days you are doing something sober, without your 'friend' and prop, alcohol, either for the first time, or for the first time for many years. Getting through each day sober is a success worthy of a medal. I took a decision to avoid all possible life events while I was getting used to life without alcohol and surprised myself when I managed a whole year event free. It did cross my mind that perhaps I had chosen some of the destabilising 'events' in my life as an excuse for drinking.

In 1988, I had become vegetarian and so had some experience of explaining to people that I didn't eat meat. Now I tried to use a similar simple explanation about not drinking alcohol. Most people were fine with the 'no meat' thing but it was not the same for alcohol. 'Just one glass won't hurt' or 'are you on tablets?' Then I could see Roger tensing up because he knew that I would now reveal that I am an alcoholic. Then there followed the stony silence and often the 'no you are not' response. I didn't argue. I just waited until the next stage; the subject may be dropped or someone next to me may have started talking in secretive hushed tones while everyone else talked loudly about the weather. Or, there may have been a full-blown attack in which the wine pourer refused to accept my 'no' and just carried on pouring. Some people just saw my statement as an affront on their own drinking habit, which it was not.

Quite often, there was an embarrassed joke about twelve step programmes that fell flat and finally, everyone moved on to more neutral subjects.

Are you ready for the answer?
I learnt when I was working as a GP, that on the whole, people ask a question about a difficult subject when they are ready to hear the answer. I think this is also true of alcoholism and sobriety. People ask me about it when they need the information. I have found that often friends have to deal with the someone's problem drinking and do not know where to turn for advice. I have had numerous conversations about the boundary between heavy drinking and addiction to alcohol, and about how the partner of the drinker can tread the delicate line between enabling and challenging damaging behaviour. There are no right answers but there are common sense boundaries.

I had decided not to try to stop smoking at the same time as stopping drinking alcohol. Three years later, I was working as Director of Public Health in Surrey and managing the Health Promotion Unit. We had adjacent offices. It was brought to my attention that visitors who came to collect 'stop smoking' packs had to endure a corridor of stale smoke on the way. I could not defend it any longer and decided to stop smoking. I found it harder than stopping drinking.

Chapter 8

My watch again

In August 1998, our friends Mike and Mary, signed up to sail around the world as part of the Blue Water Rally that would begin in 1999. The first leg would be sailing to Tenerife. They invited Roger and me to join them for the Atlantic leg from Tenerife to Antigua. Roger accepted immediately. Having read the log of Roger's Atlantic crossing in February 1997, I was reluctant, but they said they would be crossing further south in November when the gentle trade winds would waft their boat, Meriva, across the Atlantic. It would just be a question of setting the sails and putting our feet up, they said. No thanks, I said.

Meriva, a forty-two-foot Bermuda rig sloop built in 1968, was moored in Mount Batten Marina in Plymouth, as was our boat, Novara. Although she was a beautiful boat Meriva needed several sections of her timber hull to be replaced. As work progressed, I became engaged with preparations for the trip, even though I was not going. I started to wonder whether perhaps I wouldn't be seasick, or it might gradually wear off during the trip. Mike and Mary jumped on this sign of weakness and said they would not invite anyone else to crew until I have had plenty of time to think about it. Six months was mentioned as thinking time. I gave in after six weeks and agreed to join them, on the basis that it sounded like an adventure that was too good to miss. Most of my friends looked at me as though I had gone mad when I told them.

In preparation, I qualified as a day skipper and four months later a 'Survival at Sea' course. The theory part was not cheering, with a video of dead people on an upturned life raft in the North Sea and exhortations that they would have stood a chance of survival if they had turned it the right way up and got under cover. For the practical session, we had to wear all our normal day clothes plus foul weather gear, including deck boots and an inflated life jacket then jump into a swimming pool. Even in a warm swimming pool with no waves, it was very difficult to breathe or to follow instructions to join hands with the others for safety.

The instructors had made their point, as far as I was concerned, but now I was expected to right a small upside-down life raft. I managed that, but getting into it took all my strength, endurance and determination. Face down inside, with my nose in a foetid puddle, my inflated life jacket somehow got wedged and it would have been easy to drown. I would not qualify until I had completed the next task – hauling an unconscious person who was heavier than me, into the raft. This seemed an impossible task, but they showed me the trick to it, and it was actually slightly easier than getting into the raft myself. Mary later admitted that she could not get into the raft on her course and therefore failed. She seemed quite happy about that, but I started to wonder.

Blue Water Rally held seminars to help us to prepare for a safe trip. The talk on weather was interesting but I didn't understand it. Slides of the South Sea Islands looked idyllic but were there to warn us about foundering on coral reefs, not swimming with sharks and not so sit on beaches because of crocodiles. This rather left looking at sunsets as the main source of enjoyment.

Meriva left the UK in July 1999 with Mike, Mary and two other sets of crews on the legs to Gibraltar and then Tenerife. I had been having almost continuous migraines and tried taking sanomigran to prevent them but kept dropping things and was so sleepy that I couldn't drive, so abandoned that idea. My preparations to fly out to Tenerife to join the boat in October involved packing twelve pairs of knickers, ten Weigh and Save dried cake mixes and a small pile of Kendal Mint Cake for the grab bag. It was now a year since I had done any navigation practice so I sincerely hoped that no-one would be relying on my skills to find our way across the Atlantic.

Tenerife seemed hot after a UK November. We took a coach trip around the island and visited Mount Teide volcano. The heat made sleep difficult, as did the 1,000 megawatt acid party on the town quay across the harbour that went on until 7.30am. Mike went up the mast to repair the steaming light while Mary cooked supper and I sorted out and stowed our medical supplies. On our last day in port, we bought perishable provisions and stowed those, plus extra canisters of diesel. We filled the water tanks and refuelled, and the boys completed the engine maintenance. Mike took us all through the safety at sea procedures and we checked out at customs. One rally boat has already sailed so that they could reach Antigua in time for the charter boat week. They reported very little wind. Apparently, it was a bit early for the trade winds, but they were expected the week after.

On the eighteenth of November, we set sail. Like a well-oiled machine and were first out of the harbour. There was a good wind, but it was a bit choppy. I was sick twenty minutes later. I spent twenty-four hours feeling like death and vomited every time I sat up. They began to realise how wise my original decision to stay at home had been. On our third night at sea, Mike threw Roger and me out of bed so that he could get to the manual bilge pump under our bunk. While frantically pumping, he explained that we were at danger of sinking because the automatic bilge pump had packed up and the engine compartment had filled with sea water. By the time they had pumped all the water out, both Mike and Roger were seasick. In spite of that, the floorboards came up and they spent the next day mending the automatic bilge pump.

Chinatown, the boat that is part of the rally but left a week early, radioed the rest of the fleet to say that they were out of fuel. There had been so little wind that they had had to motor continuously and were flopping about at forty degrees west. Hurricane Lennie had gone through ten days before and had disrupted the usual weather patterns. Mary was the only person on Meriva with any interest in food. Some of the fresh stuff was going off and some pears had made a break for freedom in the forepeak, where they would rot if we didn't find them, but no-one felt well enough to go in there. By our fourth night sailing, I had recovered sufficiently to want to continue living and to do my share on watch. Night watch started at 8pm when it got dark and we did two hours in rotation so in theory, we each got six hours off to sleep in between. In practice, sharing one big cabin space below decks meant that we were constantly woken by people coming on and off watch, changing in and out of clothes, shining torches on instruments and working at the navigation station.

We were steering between 240 and 270 degrees, so the sun rose almost directly behind us and flooded the sky with pink. By 10am it was so hot that we were glad to be under the bimini for our turn on steering.

A blue whale joined us at 11.45am and swam closer and closer, going from one side of the boat to the other. He seemed very interested in the trailing generator we call Sparky. This whale was very long and sleek, and very agile.

He swam under Sparky's thirty-metre rope and across our bow. Just when we thought he had gone, he reappeared spouting and swimming really close, apparently to look at us. After an hour of this, we decided to pull in Sparky in case it was annoying the whale, but he stayed with us for another hour, then started swimming under the boat for fun, like a dolphin. We adjudged that if he got his calculations slightly wrong during this manoeuvre, it would not be fun for us as he was bigger and longer than our boat - we were forty-two feet long and he looked more than fifty feet! Do whales know their own strength? We turned the engine on, as this is supposed to stop whales coming too close, but our whale had not heard this theory. He carried on swimming alongside us, but now on his side, so we could see the white of his belly. After about two hours, he swam off, probably bored.

Mary washed our hair, making sure that no-one cheated on the amount of water used. She collected the rinse water in a bowl for washing knickers later, then we had a foot inspection. Mike gave Roger a close crew cut, and Roger had a shave. Mundane acts, but when there is just you, the boat, the weather and the Atlantic, these things become important.

On day six, the engine wouldn't start. Mike and Roger lifted the floor and spent the day in the engine space. I told Mary that I had heard the same sound when the Bendix went on my Mini Cooper. The men narrowed the problem down to the starter motor that was probably unhappy about having been flooded with sea water on day three.

Reg and Phil on Mr Bean (their boat) started a fleet entertainment channel they call Radio Calypso at 6.30 each evening where we broadcast for help with the starter motor. Men on other boats diagnosed a problem with the Bendix, which was now an acceptable diagnosis because they were men. The knowledge didn't help though, as it was inaccessible under the floorboards. To save power, we turned off the fridge and water pump and stopped using lights inside the cabin apart from the instrument lights at night. Then we lost Sparky, the trailing generator, and our only source of power. His rope either snagged on something or overheated. Anyway, it was gone.

Roger had a lot of sailing experience and knew all about setting the sails, which was reassuring, given that we were now likely to have to sail all the way without our engine. This was a pretty scary idea to me, and I felt anxious, since we were now beyond the reach of air rescue (500 miles) but I gradually got used to things not working. My worst moment was alone on night watch when a flying fish landed on my bare neck and flapped about.

We were doing about 120 miles a day and had passed our 'quarter of the way there' distance of 650 miles, so we had a party on board that night to celebrate. Next day the wind changed direction. The boat was over at fifteen degrees and we were constantly buffeted by the waves, so we had to hang on when moving about which was a problem if you were trying to carry anything. We were all feeling ill again. I was worst and could not stand the sight or smell of food but if I didn't eat, I got dizzy and that was dangerous.

Safety was a higher priority now that we did not have an engine. After dark, everyone had to wear a life jacket and hook on. We were careful to keep ropes coiled and ready for use. Mary checked that each of us is drinking one and a half litres of water every twenty-four hours. It was easy to overlook. We brought plenty of drinking water with us.

Day eight was too rough to fish and an untidy sea. Roger listened to World Service for the football results. He said he was having a nice time.

On day nine, we used some precious battery power to have our moment of glory singing 'my starter motor lies over the ocean' on Radio Calypso. We were very nervous and did a lot of rehearsing, but it went well. By day ten we were half-way there and I saw two shooting stars on night watch.

On day eleven we were becalmed. Roger spent the morning fishing and caught a wahoo which he cooked for lunch. It was delicious. In the afternoon, there was a sharp rain shower, so Roger had a shave (hooray) and we got some of the salt off our skin. We also gave the cockpit a spring clean with sea water. Mary's housekeeping schedule had this day as the day for us to cut our fingernails and handed round the clippers. Roger and I got a clean top sheet for our bunk – not a moment too soon – and I was allowed some water to wash my knickers again, so feeling very spruce and smart.

Watches were quite business-like. Apart from maintaining the course, every ten minutes we did a 360-degree check on the horizon for other boats to make sure we were not on a collision course. We had only seen one cruise liner so far. They could appear over the horizon and be with you in thirty minutes. We had limited manoeuvrability without an engine so were concerned when we knew that The Arcadia, a huge cruise ship, was in the vicinity and had asked all small boats to display navigation lights as they were not sure they can pick us up on radar. We radioed them to give our position and to tell them of our restricted ability to manoeuvre due to loss of engine. They responded very sympathetically, called Mike 'Sir,' slowed down to twenty knots and changed course to be sure of missing us by three miles. We saw them go past. It was a VERY big boat with thousands of lights on so of course, the crew would have no night vision.

The boat called Sabbatical joined us at 7.50pm for a mid- Atlantic exchange. They gave us their spare trailing generator and extra drinking water, and we gave them our fuel as it is of no use without the engine.

The wind dropped off badly on day fourteen, so it was a noisy night with the sails flapping and the boom rattling. At 7am, the wind went completely, and fifteen dolphins came to play around our prow. The cruising shute went out and we got three knots of boat speed. Ours was a 2,800-mile journey and most boats were carrying enough fuel for 800 miles of motoring. When becalmed they had to judge whether to use some of their fuel to use their motor or wait for the wind. There was a lot of waiting.

On day thirteen, our first one-hundred litre tank of water was empty. We still had two other tanks that contained a total of one hundred and sixty-five litres, another fifty litres in plastic containers as well as 230 litres of drinking water. Mary had planned well. We sailed into a thunderstorm and the wind picked up at an alarming rate. It happened so quickly that it wasn't safe to get the sails in. Mary steered Meriva like a bobsled on the Cresta run. Cowering in my bunk, I sensed danger and forced myself on deck. Suddenly the sail split with a bang and the shreds dangled in the water. Mike rushed to the prow and dragged the soggy remains on board. He and Roger stuffed it into a sailing bag and spent twenty minutes in raging seas sorting out the sheets (ropes) that had wrapped themselves around the forestay. At this point, Mary (still helming the Cresta run) and I (petrified but cool) observed that we were doing four knots of boat speed without any sails at all. When Roger and Mike got back to the cockpit, we sang 'always look on the bright side of life' and ate fruit cake for a late lunch.

Where are the trade winds?
During the early hours of day fifteen, the wind speed dropped to zero. This sort of thing infuriates sailors like Roger and Mike who were not happy people when there was no wind. They insisted on leaving the mainsail up 'in case' so wind arrived but the flapping noise it made was unbearable, so it was furled. After that, we flopped around with just the triangle of genoa for the rest of the night.

It was hot. I had not anticipated being too hot in mid Atlantic. We were all tired too. Squabbles broke out. We sent Mike and Roger to their bunks to catch up on sleep. Mike's quote of the day was 'never complain about a south westerly because going in the wrong direction is better than going nowhere.' Mary cooked delicious scones for tea.

Next day, Mike made toasted cheese for lunch, which was delicious, despite the cheese being a bit soggy now – it had been in a plastic bag in a bucket of lukewarm water for thirteen days. With renewed energy, Mike then lifted the floorboards and put his head in the engine compartment to take off the solenoid and starter motor. He had to saw off a bit of boat to get access. He dried the solenoid and hit the starter motor with a hammer, but it didn't make them work. We asked if we could hit it too.

We were only making sixty miles a day in light winds and falling behind the fleet because they could motor in the windless times. I felt well enough to prepare my first meal; vegetarian spaghetti bolognaise and a ginger cake. I felt proud.

On day seventeen, the wind died again on my watch at 5am. I was feeling rather persecuted because it always waited until my watch to do this and then we would have a noisy sleepless night with no progress, and I felt responsible. I had thought the moon would be there to give us light on dark nights. But no. It just appeared when it felt like it and had hardly been around at all for a week. On the previous night, it appeared in a pathetic state above a cloud at 4.30am just before the sun came up. Useless thing.

I made porridge for breakfast to cheer us up on day eighteen and Mary did her Christmas cards so that they would be ready for someone to take to the UK to post when we reached Antigua. My hair was now very straggly, having failed to get it cut before we set off and the salt treatment has made it stiff and tangled. Mike offered to cut it for me because his mum was a hairdresser and since that was the best offer, I was likely to get mid Atlantic, I let him. Roger said it looked okay.

We saw a frigate bird and I got slightly excited about being near to land but apparently, we were not. We were at 44 degrees west and Antigua is 61 degrees west so that left 17.5 degrees to go. One degree is equivalent to fifty-four miles at our altitude. One-degree north is sixty miles wherever you are. I didn't make the rules about that. We were gaily saying 'only 1,000 miles to go' whereas two weeks ago, we would have spent a week planning a sixty-mile channel crossing.

That night, we had a vegetable pie and a pudding of tinned raspberries and evaporated milk with meringues. And to top it off, a quiz night before my 10pm to midnight watch started. The wind did not drop all night. In fact, it went screaming up to twenty knots, giving us six knots of boat speed. Roger knew that I was nervous about this sort of speed and came up to help me without being asked, which was lovely of him and reassuring as he had the 12-2am watch. We shared the four-hour watch with one hour on and one off, the 'off' person lying down in the cockpit. The wind settled down to a steady level allowing us to get up to the sort of naughtiness for which there isn't space in our bunk. Towards 2am the wind dropped again, and the sails were flapping again. At least there was cloud cover, so we were not baking hot. Being Sunday, we played hymns on the cassette recorder and sang along, as you do.

We had come to the end of the sliced white bread we had bought in huge quantity in Tenerife. It was called Bimbo on the wrapper, but we forgave it because it lasted so well. I made bread for the first time on board. We needed the wind to pick up because the trailing generator didn't work at low speeds, so our battery power was well down.

On day nineteen, Mike called for help at 5am. Mary took over the helm, shivering in her nightie and drenched with rain. We were in the middle of a big squall. Roger battled to shorten the genoa in raging seas. At some point, I heard him say 'the lazy sheet has gone over the side.' He crawled forward to grab it, but it hit him on the head twice. Eventually he and Mike were back in the cockpit holding the genoa sheet, both wet through. I made hot drinks for us all while Mary changed into dry clothes. By the time it was my watch, the wind had picked up to the extent that I was in a panic and shouting, 'GOING TOO FAST.' But the rest of the crew were really happy that we were on the move and sent me away.

Some of the sailing boats of the annual ARC race crossed our course mid Atlantic. At noon, there was grim news on the net. A nearby Norwegian yacht in the ARC had lost a man overboard at 4am. Sabbatical, two other Norwegian yachts and an American naval vessel were involved in the search. We were not in the search area.

Other boats in the Blue Water fleet were sailing rather than motoring to save fuel so we were catching them up. One had reached Antigua and said that the weather was awful with torrential rain. They warned us not to approach Falmouth Harbour at night as it was a difficult approach and the markers had been torn away during a recent hurricane.

I went to bed early in anticipation of a disturbed night and sure enough, just after eight, I sensed SPEED and had to stick my head up onto the cockpit and shout, 'TOO FAST'. Mike rushed past me, throwing his safety harness into the cockpit and for an hour and a half he and Roger battled raging seas, torrential rain and howling wind in a total blackout. Twice the GPS registered a boat speed of just over eleven knots. This is not the sort of sailing they said it would be. I was on watch from 2am but a big black cloud sent the wind speed soaring to twenty knots and I had to call Roger to helm as I wasn't strong enough to hold it. It was a night of one squall after another and by 5.45am I was falling asleep at the helm.

Day twenty was our last full Tuesday at sea. We were three quarters of the way there, so we had a three quarters of the way party. Another shower provided water for a welcome hair wash which was always good when you had a party to go to. Mike lost his watch over the side while attending to ropes. It was the one his children bought him for his fiftieth, which was sad. A white egret tried to land on us, and we got lots of clothes dry, which is important at sea.

I cooked vegetable risotto and satay sauce for supper and got an ocarina for my three-quarters-of- the-way present – a hand carved pottery one that Mary had bought in La Gomera. I didn't really feel in a party mood though as I was very tired and kept thinking about the Norwegian man overboard.

I went to bed early and by the time it was my watch, we were becalmed again. I sat at the wheel disconsolately for the rest of my watch, unable to stop us drifting around in circles. When I completed the log at midnight, we had drifted backwards a mile, which was dispiriting. I would have quite like to be on dry land.

On day twenty-two, my watch started at 6am and we were going forward slowly. Roger decided to hoist the main to use what wind there was, but the boom started flapping everywhere so I couldn't steer, and I burst into tears. Mike rushed up and took the mainsheet and patted my hand reassuringly. Roger appeared in the cockpit and made things worse by asking, 'what's the matter?' How could he not know? This is the most truly awful experience I have ever had including my hysterectomy, and he is asking what the matter is. I had lost all perspective and was sent to bed for a good cry and a cuddle with Roger. I just needed a couple of hours with the boat going in the right direction and nothing terrifying happening. Roger could not understand because for him there had not been anything frightening. Later there was great news. A yacht had found the Norwegian man overboard alive and well. Only 585 miles to go.

At last, on day twenty-three we had a quiet night and enough wind for us to be able to hold our course. There were things suspiciously like trade wind clouds around and we had a good sailing day. On watch from midnight to 2am, I had to deal with high winds and a choppy sea, but I was getting better at helming. Then the toilet seat broke. I wanted to go home.

On day twenty-four, Mike shaved his beard off and looked less scary. Many of our Blue Water Rally boats had arrived in Antigua. Once within 500 miles, they had been using their engines. Mary made bread and for supper I cooked chilli sans carne and carrot cake with pineapple which was horrible. Even the men wouldn't eat it. I was now terminally tired.

On day twenty-six, Mike furled the headsail right down and took a reef in for the night to slow us down and delay our arrival at Falmouth Harbour. At the speed we were doing we would have arrived at 4am and have had to wait for dawn before we could dock. Consequently, we had another night of flapping and flopping around and not much sleep.

At dawn on day twenty-seven, we passed Guadeloupe on our port side and then saw Monserrat and St Kits through the mist. As the sun came up, the hills of Antigua turned from grey to green. It was so good to see green again. A cloud drifted over, we had a few drops of rain, then a small rainbow right in front of us, its tail dipping into Falmouth Harbour.

Roger helmed us between rows of moored boats. Mike dropped the sail for the last time and took a tow rope. Mary and I rushed fenders to port and starboard as we slid into a mooring on the Antigua Yacht Club pontoon.

Once off Meriva, there were hugs from everyone in the Blue Water fleet who had followed our engineless progress with some concern. We had done it. Good old Meriva. Cold beer and orange juice, even some champagne and fresh croissants arrived.

It was strangely unreal to be on shore after such a long trip. We had put the needs of the boat first for twenty-six days and it was difficult to stop thinking like that. The boat seemed to have more personality than the crew and it felt quite wrong to just leave her – almost like leaving a child without a minder.

Tired as we were, we had essential jobs to do before resting. I took five black bags to the rubbish tip leaving Terry, the engineer, attacking the starter motor. We booked the blown-out cruising chute for repair at the sail makers' and sent off the first load of washing. While the engineer had the floorboards up, we went in search of an Antiguan driving licence for Mike and then a hire car before relaxing at the beach bar. Several skippers and crew agreed that there was not much to recommend the Atlantic crossing in the absence of trade winds. My sentiments entirely. On some boats, the crew had walked off as soon as they docked and were not talking to their skipper. We felt quite proud that we had all stayed friends on Meriva despite the ups and downs.

We called the family before getting ready for the Blue Water beach party at Jolly Harbour. We had to take the inland route because Hurricane Lennie had washed away the coast road. Our drive took us past damaged tin huts, goats, chickens, potholes and many speed bumps but no signposts. The party was on the beach, where we paddled and watched Monserrat with its smoking volcano until sunset. Paddling was the first time we had actually had our feet in the Atlantic.

Chapter 9

Listening for the skylarks

In 1995, there were plans to amalgamate District Health Authority (DHA) where I worked, with the DHA next door. Having had experience of previous NHS reorganisations I had a fair idea what would happen: all management posts would be declared redundant and advertised. There would be interviews, new appointments, restructuring and then jostling for position in the senior management group. In the meantime, there would be a leadership and policy vacuum. The Chairman clarified the timing of the redundancy of the senior management posts in a bad photocopy of a fax that was not personally addressed. I thought we deserved better than that. I spent time arranging for my staff to find new placements and did not reapply for my job. I left without a backward glance and only went back into work briefly to take a chocolate cake to the IT team and rewrite the specification for communicable disease control.

On the first of April 1995, I had my first un-jobbed day. It was a beautiful sunny spring morning and I woke at 7am because I had forgotten to turn the radio alarm off. I listened for the news item that would be an April Fool but decided it could be all or none of them. I spent the morning at the park with our granddaughter where we tried to hit Canadian Geese with lumps of bread.

Most days, I found myself doing things that I used to keep for weekends: washing, cleaning, shopping, moving furniture around and doing several miles' cycling on days when it was not raining. I decided to return to General Practice and applied for a six-month training post. It was many years since I had worked as a clinical doctor and during that time, several new diseases had been invented, many drugs taken off prescription and they had decimalised laboratory test results. I chose a practice that had been computerised and caught up sufficiently to feel that I could practice safely. For the next three years, I did GP locums.

In March 1996, Roger took early retirement and spent most of the summer sailing. His mum had died, but his dad still lived in Plymouth and was becoming frail. My parents had retired to Seaton in Devon and also had failing health. After a succession of frantic trips to Devon to provide crisis support, we realised that they needed more and that we would have to live closer to them, even though this would mean the creation of a huge distance between us and our beloved children and grandchildren. So, in an eventful October in 1996, we moved to Devon in the same week that Roger's daughter, Claire, married Dominic in Cornwall.

Village life

We bought a converted barn with eight acres of land. We had no idea what was involved in managing eight acres of land, so Roger went out and bought a boat and I stood for the Parish Council. It all got a bit hectic. Our new kitchen had a large AGA but nothing else. We dined off the plastic garden furniture we had brought from London through that first winter while we decided what sort of kitchen we would like and found someone to build it. Claire and Dom spent that winter planning a long trip to Australia and after Christmas, Roger accepted an invitation to sail the Atlantic on a Chay Blyth crossing. By April 1997, I had the place to myself.

We had always done our own home decorating but work in the barn was a whole new ballpark. The electric drill that had worked fine in our London house, was not man enough for the job when the walls are built using local stone. It just slid off the walls and we had to buy a more powerful one to get curtain poles up. The Great Hall was forty feet long and we needed tower scaffold to make the gable end weatherproof and decorate it. The developer had used the wrong render so that had to be removed and replaced with a lime plaster. We could reach the beams to the gabled roof to wire in the speakers but anything above that we left for the spiders. Occasional inspections at dizzying heights to check on electric cables, revealed straw and grains on the rafters from the hall's previous life.

The two acres of ground around the barn turned out to be devoid of topsoil, lost when the area was landscaped. We brought in a dozen ten ton loads from a local building site but even that did not quite cover it. Roger created raised beds so that we could become self-sufficient, and there ensued several summers' worth of 'debate' about whether I was allowed to grow plants there that I could use to dye wool. Roger morphed from insurance broker into a man with a sit on mower and a quad bike.

We began to volunteer at a community event in north Cornwall, helping during the annual week's camp there each summer where there were intensive workshops to learn straw bale building, yurt making, iron age smelting, basketmaking, yoga, coracle making. There was also a range of activities more suitable for children who rushed through their hand cooked evening meal, to storytelling round the campfire. We learnt to shave and bend poles to make a yurt and after a week of particularly bad weather that include watching waterspouts approach from the sea, we abandoned our tent and bought a yurt for the following summer, part of which we made ourselves.

After our momentous Atlantic crossing with Mike and Mary over the millennium, Roger was ripe for another long sailing trip and in 2001, he joined a friend's boat in Sri Lanka to act as crew. Their route would include crossing the Indian Ocean where there was a lot of Somalian pirate activity at the time. The boats on the rally had to maintain radio silence and I worried when the date for their landfall passed with no word. Then, to my relief, the phone rang. 'I am in Djibouti,' said Roger. 'Can you call me back? It's a public holiday and everything is closed, so this kind man has let me call from his café.' He gave me the number and rang off. I grabbed the book of international phone codes, then thought, 'Where the fuck is Djibouti?' I finally established that Djibouti is both a town and a country and found the code. All was well. They then sailed on up the Red Sea to the Mediterranean.

I took a City and Guilds course in basketry, another in upholstery and learnt to spin, there being a steady local supply of Jacobs' fleece at that time. Friends had lent us their sheep to keep the grass down but when there was an outbreak of Foot and Mouth disease locally, all animal movements were banned because our fields were contiguous with the farm next to an infected herd. If it came any closer, all human movements would stop as well. Our village was un-naturally quiet, tense and sad-and-angry at the same time, with slaughtered animals piled up in full view nearby. I was cross because I knew that the government had been too slow to react to the outbreak and had then taken steps that were not scientifically valid, just as had happened with BSE. God save us from politicians who do not respect scientific evidence. We had agreed that I would fly out to Crete to meet Roger with a bag of replacement parts for the boat. I had my suitcase packed and ready and, in the end, human movements were not restricted in our area, so I was able to get to Heathrow.

Parish councillor for burials

It took five years living in Devon for the pattern of the seasons to feel normal. We hadn't really noticed seasons much in London. When we were living in towns, I thought that I was a true environmentalist and was violently anti-hunting, but a number of local events in Devon persuaded me otherwise. I could see how our landowners and farmers did their best for wildlife and that hunting was part of our local culture. Whilst I did not want to join a hunt (horses do not like me), I came to believe that it is important to keep the tradition going.

Soon after our Atlantic crossing, I was co-opted onto the local Parish Council. Here, I learnt new and strange things, like the law on Public Footpaths, formation of Karst holes in our village, planning law and emergency planning at local level. Our council undertook a survey of every household so that we could draw up a Parish Plan. One of the things people said was important to them, was to be able to be buried within the parish when they died. Our local churchyard had just been closed to new business because it was full. The alternatives available to us now were either burial within the boundaries of Plymouth or cremation. As I read about cremation, I realised that it was not good for the environment, considering the amount of fuel required to achieve temperatures that were a legal requirement, and the amount of heavy metal released into the air.

Thus, I became the lead councillor for burials. I was influenced by my recent diploma course in Permaculture and keen to find a way to open a natural burial ground for local people. I started with the vicar, who advised me that it would never happen because the Church of England Bishop in Exeter was very influential and would block any planning application. He was said to have an intense and unshakeable dislike of natural burial grounds. I heard about a young woman who had been successful in obtaining a huge government grant to buy a field in Walkhampton on Dartmoor, so that she could open a natural burial ground. When I went to see her, it was clear that there was so much local opposition that her burial ground was unlikely to open. She was downhearted, but I had learnt a lot: get the support of local people for the idea and set up a steering group composed of local religious and political leaders.

Before we went any further, we checked the level of support for a natural burial ground. 68% of respondents said they would consider using a natural burial ground if there was one within easy reach and 78% said they would consider using it if they were organising someone else's funeral. We decided to go ahead.

Our steering group included local leaders for the Church of England and the Methodist Church. Both were respected and influential in our community and used to working together. They were supportive of the proposal to open a natural burial ground and educated the rest of us on the relevance of consecration of the ground. Apparently, when you consecrate a piece of ground, it is consecrated to one religion. This would severely limit the number of potential customers. Instead, we adopted a policy of welcoming people from all religions and encouraged individual graves to be blessed rather than consecrated.

We planned to leave most of the 3.85-hectare field as meadowland grazed by sheep until it filled up a bit. Those sheep needed stock fencing but would obviate the need for frequent mechanical mowing. There were not many natural burial grounds to refer to in 2002, but we visited those we could find in the south west. In the longer term, when full of graves, our aim was for the burial ground to become a woodland in perpetuity, and relatives would be encouraged to plant a tree in memory of the deceased.

We invited two local funeral directors to one of our meetings to explain our aims and plans, and to get their reaction to our proposals. They would be the gateway between grieving relatives and our new business. On the whole, they thought our ideas fairly good although not at all what they were used to, and they expressed doubts about how many people would be ready for such a radical change. We had not thought of ourselves as radical until then. However, we learnt a lot about how to approach funeral directors and they gave us sound advice on practical things, such as how far it is possible to carry a heavy coffin over rough ground. They said that many relatives want to visit a grave fairly frequently after the burial, and on the first anniversary, but after that many come to terms with their loss and when five years have passed, few visit the grave with any frequency.

I undertook the environmental assessment required for planning consent, which seemed straightforward. But the Environment Agency was feeling particularly vulnerable at this time, owing to criticisms of the manner of disposal of carcasses during the outbreak of Foot and Mouth Disease.

They suggested that 'the proposed change of use has the potential to impact on ground water quality.' Since the field is on a hill, half a mile above the river, this seemed excessive, but when I got into the detail, I understood that with some geological formations pollution, can drain into an underground basin from which drinking water is extracted miles away. Fortunately, we could prove that the rainwater from the field drained straight into the River Yealm at a point beyond any possible abstraction of drinking water.

We had to prove to the Environment Agency that there was good drainage, although there had not, at that time, been any relevant studies in the UK to suggest what drainage there should be and there have been few studies of the effect of leachate from cemeteries into ground water. A friendly farmer brought a tractor and digger in so that I could measure the rate of percolation and I provided them with vital information such as our annual rainfall (40 inches) and the composition of a typical human body (64% water). Apparently, over half the decomposition of a human corpse occurs within the first year.

Nobody talks about death in England. People running cemeteries have more or less been left to sort themselves out and many ran into difficulty in the 1960s, because their cemeteries were full. Once full, they have no further income and some companies locked the gates and simply walked away for good: Highgate Cemetery and Nunhead Cemetery were effectively abandoned until local groups decided to find a way out of the impasse.

This may be part of the reason that cremations became more Popular than burials. The UK has the highest rate of cremations in the world (70% as opposed to 30% burials).

450,000 coffins were burnt every year in the UK, releasing dioxins, acids, mercury and carbon dioxide. Our woodland burial ground would offer an environmentally preferable option.

Our burial ground opened in 2003 and is going well. Several hundred people including members of our family have since been buried there and the trees are resplendent.

One of the most satisfying days was observing a funeral in bright sunlight, with hares lurking in the undergrowth and skylarks singing overhead.

170

Epilogue

The problem with portraits

What do other people think of us? I worried endlessly about this as a teenager. When I was twenty-one, studying medicine and looking after my first baby, there was no longer time for such worry. I felt much better and decided to carry on with not worrying. In fact, I gave up worrying altogether, as far as possible. It is a waste of time!

Now in my seventies, I had not considered what others thought of me until writing this memoir. Occasionally, people have made comments. For instance, my dear friend Sally said that the thing she admired most was the fact that I am authentic. I had to ask her what that meant, but then I quite liked the idea. When I left a job in London and took one in Surrey, Mariella (a colleague) gasped and said, 'Is Surrey ready for you?'. More recently Keith's wife described me as 'nice'. I liked Keith's response: 'Linda is many things, but nice is not one of them'. And Liz Shore, with whom I worked in London described me as having 'a mind like a steel trap'. I hope this book doesn't disillusion any of them.

Writing this memoir, looking back at my life, I have been reminded of some of the really big lessons I have had to learn. These lessons are not in any particular order.

There are all sorts of love, but I think the most important is the unconditional kind of love. I learnt that as long as you are bathed in plenty of this as a child, it doesn't matter where it comes from. My store of unconditional love came from my Nanna and Pop. I have sometimes fallen out with people who use conditional love as a parenting tool. That was never my way.

The placebo effect is one of the best healers and comes without side effects. I was never a 'do as I say' kind of GP but did become aware that patients do better if they have confidence in their doctor, and so developed a clinical persona that was a gentle mix of authority and concern. After some years, this became so ingrained that it intruded into other relationships. People would see me as a doctor first and a person second. Judith, a colleague made a wise suggestion. Stop saying 'I am a doctor' and start saying 'I work as a doctor'. This made a huge difference.

On the other hand, I have been known to play the doctor card to my advantage. I was cured of this when stuck behind a huge delivery van in Sheffield. 'I am a doctor. You will have to move because I need to get to a patient.' 'I don't care if you are two doctors,' he said, 'I can't move until the one in front has unloaded'. Arrogance rarely pays off!

I always wanted to be a GP, but no-one had taught me about boundaries. As a result, when patients were sad or in pain, I empathised to the extent that eventually I felt 'used up'. Alcohol is an unrivalled way of numbing emotional pain and this worked for me for some years. But in the end, something had to give, so I changed to a non-clinical career path (Public Health) and abstinence. Studying for the exams was a challenge after a long gap, and there turned out to be quite a large gap between theory and practice. It is fair to say that over the next ten years, I never took a job that I could already do. I encourage all women to adopt this as a personal policy – men already do! A large part of Public Health work involves encouraging people to change, to a healthier lifestyle or to audit the work they do. I learnt that to encourage change, you need to start where they are, not to harangue them with visions of what they might eventually achieve. It is all about respect.

There were years of tumult in my life. I finally learnt that I actually prefer peace, and that happiness is a by-product of how you live, not something separate. I believe in Scott Peck's view that we are here to learn, and so good and bad experiences are equally useful.

While trying to put all of these lessons into practice, as time passes, I am still learning retirement skills. The main requirement is to be adaptable. Parts of the body become unreliable, so we have downsized and moved into the village. Remaining conscious of the imperative that we are here to learn, I have mastered basketmaking, upholstery, singing barbershop and spinning wool. Creative writing is a work in progress. Oh. And dogs. We always had cats while we were working. They came everywhere with us, especially on our trips on canal boats. When Roger was seventy, I bought him a pedigree black Labrador. He is called Saba. Learning about owning a dog (you have to walk him HOW often?) has been just the most life enhancing and fun, new skill of retirement. Then there is the balance to be struck about how much to be involved in the lives of our children and grandchildren. Friendships acquire enhanced importance when there is so much distance between us and our family.

We travel less. This is partly due to having already been everywhere, partly because we don't want to leave the dog, but mainly because we came to realise the effect air travel has on the climate. We live in Devon, which is one of the best holiday destinations in the world and we welcome a regular flow of visitors. At least we do when the trains are running. The railway line through Dawlish has never coped well with bad weather, and there doesn't seem to be a politically acceptable solution.

New Year resolutions now relate to getting our house in order: keeping the will up to date, registering a lasting power of attorney, that sort of thing. We have seen how gut wrenchingly awful it is when someone dies without leaving a will. And clearing out STUFF. When our parents died, it was difficult making decisions about what to keep, what to throw and what to recycle. Our children and executors will have to deal with that, but we would like to keep the task manageable. Apart from the wool. I need all that wool stashed away in chests and cupboards, the attic and the tops of wardrobes. Because it may come in useful. And I do like to be, useful!

There remains the problem of the portraits we had painted in the 1990s. They were a joke, to be hung in the eves of the Great Hall when we lived in a converted barn. They are huge. For six years, they have languished in storage, useless now that we have had that joke. No-one wants them. So, the plan is to take them to the funeral service (whoever dies first) and leave them there. Deliberate denigration of responsibility. And thinking of funerals gave me the idea for that novel, which is where this story ends and another begins.